D1557245

Behind
the Wall of
Respect

The University of Chicago Press
Chicago and London

Behind the Wall of Respect

Patrick H. Hughes, M.D.

Community Experiments in Heroin Addiction Control

With a Foreword by
Daniel X. Freedman, M.D.

Patrick H. Hughes, M.D., received his medical degree
(1960) from the University of Pittsburgh. He also holds an
M.S. degree (1967) from the school of Public Health, Columbia University. He served his medical internship at
Stanford Medical Center and a four-year residency in psychiatry at Columbia Presbyterian Medical Center, New York
City. Since 1968 he has taught at the University of Chicago,
where he is associate professor in the Department of Psychiatry. Currently (1976–77) on leave of absence from the
University, Dr. Hughes is working with the World Health
Organization to implement drug abuse treatment and research programs in developing countries.

The University of Chicago Press, Chicago 60637
The University of Chicago Press, Ltd., London

Library of Congress Cataloging in Publication Data

Hughes, Patrick H
  Behind the wall of respect.

  Includes bibliographical references and index.
  1. Heroin. 2. Drug abuse—Treatment—Illinois
—Chicago. 3. Halfway houses—Illinois—Chicago.
I. Title.
HV5822.H4H79   362.2'93'0977311   76-25640
ISBN 0-226-35930-1

This work was made possible by the Drug Abuse Council, Inc., of Washington, D.C. The Drug Abuse Council is a private, tax-exempt foundation which was established in February 1972 to serve on a national level as an independent source of needed research, public policy evaluation, and program guidance in the area of drug use and misuse. It is supported by the Ford Foundation, Commonwealth Fund, Carnegie Corporation, Henry J. Kaiser Family Foundation, and the Equitable Life Assurance Society of the United States.

Through its publications and other activities, the Council hopes to provide nonpartisan, objective information and analysis and serve as a resource for those organizations and individuals searching for new, more effective approaches to nonmedical drug use in our society.

Contents

Foreword

I have little doubt that in the mid-60s the vehicle for turning the attention of influential elements in our society to therapy for narcotics addiction was not only crime but the illicit use of LSD, stimulants, and, later, marihuana by the children of the culture-bearing elite. The discovery of the misuse of drugs regularly elicits the sequence of alarm, anger, blame, the search for control; it finally may seriously engage empathy and commitment to the long, hard task of coping with human need and folly. At the very least, the epidemic of drug interest in that era called upon a truly scant cadre of "experts" to explain and to engage with "drug problems." That these in fact were "people problems," that no sector of society is immune to the misuse of any drug, including the opiates such as heroin, is an infirmly but more widely appreciated fact in 1976 than in 1966. After all, in 1900 there were more addicts per capita to opiates than now, and they were by and large middle-class persons, using tonics in an era when pharmacological effects of opiates were poorly appreciated and the manufacture of medicines unregulated.

By 1971, drug misuse was clearly perceived as a public health problem—a particular set of psychosocial problems involving drugs both as a causative factor and as a component of treatment. But it was in 1965 that a few public-spirited legislators, physicians, and judges in

Illinois had mandated a treatment program for narcotic addicts. When I came to the University of Chicago's Department of Psychiatry in 1966, I was asked by Dr. Harold Visotsky, director of the state's Department of Mental Health, to bring the social-psychological and medical skills of psychiatry to focus on the problem. Jerome Jaffe, and later C. Robert Schuster, Edward Senay, and Patrick Hughes, joined the university's department to work on molecular and animal behavioral models of addiction, as well as on the design for a treatment system which could utilize, under one noncontentious umbrella, group therapies, drug-free therapeutic communities, methadone clinics, and halfway houses. The hope was to evaluate effectiveness of these various treatment modalities. The effort was unique in this country. While the group struggled to implement these programs, many national and international visitors from the range of disciplines which were becoming concerned with the task of organizing treatment programs came to observe and train.

Dr. Hughes brought a strong and specific interest in public health methodologies and, along with all of those helping to start the Illinois treatment programs, began with the first tentative and somewhat frightening search for addicts willing to enter a hospital for treatment; this was thought to be the only secure and safe way to cope with and treat these disorders. The role of the "guide"—now recognized as the ex-addict paraprofessional—was crucial in enhancing professional understanding of the addicted population and in translating the life, behaviors, and circumstance of the addict into the language of action comprehensible to a treatment team. The indispensable element for success was trust in the treatment system which was to be built, and the role of the ex-addict and treated addict was crucial in this.

With the shock of personal discovery, the human bonds forged among these personnel led to the design of outpatient clinics and treatment centers. Dr. Hughes's account of epidemiological studies poignantly tells this story of discovery, transformation, hope, and tragedy which transformed both the professionals and their paraprofessional colleagues and patients. The outcome was a design of outpatient clinics and treatment centers in an atmosphere which could, to some extent, overcome the fear and suspicion of administrators and community residents.

Hughes's retrospective analyses of Chicago's epidemics of drug use were stimulated by the patient guides. Valuable knowledge of societal perceptions, lags in community response, as well as information on the personal motives operative at various phases in the acquisition of drug habits emerged from his studies. Policy planners have not yet fully absorbed these lessons.

The use of epidemiological thought and method is clearly relevant not only to answering questions of scope and pattern of the prevailing problems, but to the vectors—the the processes such as friendship networks by which experimentation and addiction can occur. These social-psychological observations are the key to prevention.

In the startling Altgeld project, the link of epidemiology to the very invention of effective treatments and to the complete cessation of an epidemic is demonstrated. The role of community sanction and interest, of friends helping friends, of victims informing the investigators for health rather than detention purposes, were factors helping to halt an escalating and debilitating problem. Finally, without the state treatment program's openness and willingness to respond, and without the epidemiological team's link to the treatment system, Altgeld could not have happened. Had that community and its counselors and clients been able to achieve sequentially phased starter dollars for occupational rehabilitation, had they been able to implement some of their ideas for self-sustaining industry and services, the story of this project would have had a truly perfect ending.

The challenge of the studies reported here as models for formulating public health policy and programs is highlighted by some contemporary facts. Today the norm is bureaucratization of treatment rather than the excitement of collaborative discovery and hope and the capacity for flexible response from accountable public agencies. Ever new micro- and macro-epidemics recur as new generations emerge with their own climate of drug interst. Heroin use (beginning with the children of the upper middle class) is now epidemic across the globe, and for the first time in history in areas where the opium poppy is grown. Whether or not the use of a collaboration of competencies and epidemiological teams (composed of experts and guides), both for early detection and for prompt treatment response, will ever be sponsored federally or by international agencies, Dr. Hughes's account provides a useful guide. It provides as well an adventure linking science, hope, and humanism that is relevant across the span of contemporary organized health activities and "systems."

Daniel X. Freedman

Preface

Providing treatment for heroin addiction does not, by itself, assure control of the disorder. In every major city of America today, sizable programs for heroin addicts offer increasingly sophisticated medical and psychosocial treatment. But do these programs lead to fewer addicts on the streets? Do they halt spread of addiction to vulnerable young people?

Because the heroin addict subculture in any American community today is highly secretive, these questions are not readily answered. As a psychiatrist planning treatment programs for heroin addicts, I asked myself these questions. I wondered if a treatment program could really succeed in freeing entire communities from heroin addiction and, if so, how. At the corner of 43d Street and Langley Avenue on Chicago's South Side, my colleagues and I began to seek the answers.

This corner was well known in Chicago as the location of the "Wall of Respect"—actually two brick walls facing each other across Langley Avenue. Local artists had transformed them into brilliantly colored murals of rising black pride and militancy. One wall was the front of an abandoned apartment building where addicts shot up heroin and slept when they had no place to stay. Behind the other wall was a bar used by addicts as a hangout.

Behind these walls we developed our early notions of the dynamics of heroin spread and of how treatment programs might halt that process. And behind these walls we launched our first community treatment project designed to alter the addict subculture. Later we applied these approaches in other Chicago neighborhoods, each time with increasing effectiveness. The story of these community projects is the subject of this book.

Although the events to be described in the coming pages occurred in Chicago between 1968 and 1974, the scientific challenge underlying this story began some four years earlier. While fulfilling my military service obligation, I was assigned in 1964 to the addiction service of the United States Public Health Service Hospital in Fort Worth, Texas. As a psychoanalytically oriented psychiatrist, I began to treat my patients as one might expect—in individual sessions to uncover the early life events that had led to adult heroin addiction. After a few weeks, old-timers on the staff revealed with amusement that my psychotherapy patients were having much fun on the ward reporting how they were telling the new doctor exactly what he wanted to hear.

The shock and embarrassment of this event— pretty standard for newcomers to the field— taught me an important lesson; namely, what the heroin addict does in the therapist's office is not as important as what he does when he returns to his environment outside the office. At Fort Worth this environment was the addict prisoner subculture.

For two years I studied the informal dynamics of the addict patient community at Fort Worth.[1] I came to understand how the status, value, and social control systems of this community undermined all efforts of treatment staff to foster rehabilitation-oriented attitudes. In time my colleagues and I learned to manipulate that social system by exercising our power to reward individual and group behavior

in this closed and authoritarian institutional
setting.[2] But in organizing a therapeutic community in many ways similar to that of Synanon
and Daytop Village,[3] I continued to be plagued
by the inevitable relapse of our patients once
they returned to their home communities.
Whether the man was a black returning to Saint
Louis, a Mexican-American returning to San
Antonio, or a white returning to Sacramento,
the outcome was always the same. When he
passed by the old hangouts and saw his addict
friends, he could not resist the temptation to slip
back.

When I completed my assignment and returned to New York City, I toyed with the idea
of transferring to the community setting some of
the techniques I had learned at Fort Worth.
But it had been so difficult to produce and
maintain a therapeutic environment, even in an
institutional setting. How, I asked myself, could
one begin to modify the addict subculture in the
community, where the therapist holds few if any
levers of social control? But mid-1960 America
was a time and place for optimism about urban
problems. Solutions were being designed for the
"subculture of poverty" and other social ills—
why not heroin addiction as well?

To develop skills in program planning and
evaluation, to learn more about deviant subcultures, and to find out about the structure of
addiction in the urban community, I became a
student again at the Columbia University Division of Community and Social Psychiatry. This
proved fortuitous because in 1966 the field of
heroin addiction in New York City was in fer-
ment. Mayor Lindsay had just appointed Dr. Efren Ramirez to coordinate the city's addiction treatment efforts, and a major election
issue for the New York governorship was the
question of voluntary versus involuntary treatment of addicts. The Daytop Village therapeutic
community and Vincent Dole's methadone

program were both reporting initial successes, and the New York State Narcotic Addiction Control Commission had begun to acquire facilities for a massive involuntary treatment system. I remain grateful to Professors Viola Bernard, Archie Foley, and Louis Linn for making it possible for me to participate fully in the rich developments of that period through field placements with Dr. Ramirez, with Dr. Henry Brill of the New York State Narcotic Addiction Control Commission, with Dr. Marvin Perkins of the New York City Community Mental Health Board, and with the New York City probation, correction, and police departments for an intensive exposure to the many facets of addiction program planning.

During this same year I had the opportunity to study group dynamics under William Thomas and the sociology of deviance under Howard Polsky and Richard Cloward at Columbia. One day after class Professor Cloward suggested that I contact Ed Preble, an anthropologist who understood the street addict better than anyone he knew. The tip was a good one: two weeks later Ed Preble introduced me to New York's addict street subculture.

Ed Preble, who is the granddaddy of street addict researchers, arranged to meet me at a bar on 103d Street and Second Avenue in East Harlem. I was familiar with this mixed black and Puerto Rican neighborhood through my work at Block Communities, Inc. Although the block workers I supervised and the residents with whom they worked had complained a lot about addicts in the neighborhood, they had been either too fearful or not street-wise enough to provide me with access to the local addict scene.

Gaining access to the street addict was Ed Preble's business. He had a barmaid on his payroll who set up appointments with addicts Ed wanted to interview. Ed also paid an apartment owner above the bar to use her living room as an office on Saturday mornings. At the time, he was tape-recording interviews of active street addicts to collect occupational and income data. I began to accompany him on his visits to 103d Street to interview addicts and learn about the addict social system of that neighborhood. Then one Saturday Ed failed to appear. He had been hospitalized. While trying to break up a fight in that same bar several days before, he had been rewarded with a beer bottle over his skull.

The broken beer bottle incident brought my study of New York street addicts to an abrupt halt, but those few weeks with Ed Preble had been enough to help me formulate a model community treatment program for heroin addiction. The initial step in this general strategy of the program called for study of the heroin subculture of a target neighborhood in West Harlem. After identifying all active heroin users in the area, a community program would be launched to involve all addicts in treatment. The program would be successful to the degree it was able to eliminate active heroin addiction in the community.

The West Harlem proposal was not funded, so I joined the Drug Abuse Center at the National Institute for Mental Health in Washington, D.C., in 1967. There I gained useful experience in program planning and was able to integrate epidemiological and program evaluation concepts in the early Narcotic Addict Rehabilitation Act programs. But the Washington bureaucracy was not the place to learn about the practical problems of community program design, nor was it the place to innovate creative solutions to these problems. This work had to be done in the community itself.

By chance, Dr. Jerome H. Jaffe had just joined the University of Chicago to build for the State of Illinois a model treatment-research program for heroin addiction. His idea was to develop a system of clinical programs which could be experimentally manipulated to compare various approaches to treatment. I knew Jerry and told him of my interest in working with the heroin subculture for purposes of treatment program intervention. He was intrigued and invited me to Chicago to test these ideas. That is where this book begins.

Acknowledgments

Because the various projects to be described were carried out in different neighborhoods of Chicago, they involved far too many individuals to be mentioned here. Bob Rose, Clarence Lawson, and Spellmon Young, however, made special contributions which will become apparent as the story unfolds. In addition, I wish to acknowledge the special contributions of Dr. Gail A. Crawford to the conceptual evolution of the projects and for enhancing the overall scientific quality of the separate studies. I am also indebted to Richard Parker for the use of photographs from his ethnographic studies of heroin addicts in Chicago.

I am especially grateful to the chairman of the University of Chicago Psychiatry Department, Dr. Daniel X. Freedman, for his sensitivity to the needs of a developing researcher. Interdisciplinary research is difficult under the best of circumstances, but we chose a particularly difficult time for community research in Chicago. The neighborhoods we selected for projects invariably seemed to be under highly militant leadership or in great turmoil. There were periods when our projects bogged down in seemingly irreconcilable conflict or overwhelming frustration. We are all indebted to Dr. Freedman for holding us together during the many difficult periods.

The research aspects of these community projects were supported by National Institute of Mental Health and National Institute of Drug Abuse grants MH 18248 and DA 00048. I am

grateful for the many forms of assistance from
Eleanor Caroll, who served as project officer to
these grants. The State of Illinois Drug Abuse
Program provided treatment services for the
project. When Dr. Edward C. Senay followed
Dr. Jaffe as director of this program in 1971, he
took special interest in our projects, assuring
adequate treatment program support and making available his unique skill in humanizing
medical and rehabilitation services for the
addict.

The preparation of this monograph was gener-
ously supported by the Drug Abuse Council. I
am especially indebted to Dr. Thomas Bryant,
executive director of the council, for his pa-
tience and encouragement, and to Margot
Backas and Dr. Peter Bourne of the council for
their substantive and editorial suggestions to
early drafts of the manuscript. Dr. Mark
Greene and Leon Hunt of the President's
Special Action Office for Drug Abuse Prevention also made helpful suggestions to early
drafts.

Much of this book was written during a
sabbatical year at the American University in
Beirut, Lebanon, where I was fortunate to obtain the editorial assistance of Marilyn Thomas.
I am grateful for the many hours she spent
rewriting draft materials and for her suggestions
on organization and style.

Contributors

Much of the substance of this book is provided
by a series of community research projects conducted in different Chicago neighborhoods during the period 1968-74. The success of these
projects would not have been possible without
the close collaboration of a sizable team of
medical and social scientists. Nor would this
book have been written had it not been possible
to include materials and data from previously
published reports by my colleagues and me.

Where materials have been used from these earlier publications, the original references are indicated at the beginning of the respective chapters.

While I take full responsibility for the preparation of this book, I wish to acknowledge the significant contributions of Noel W. Barker to chapters 2, 3, 4, and 5; of Gail Crawford to chapters 2, 3, 4, 5, 6, and 8; of Walter Dorus to chapter 8; of Jerome Jaffe to chapters 3, 4, and 5; of Richard Parker to chapter 7; of Clinton P. Sanders and Eric S. Schaps to chapter 4; of Suzanne Schumann to chapter 3; and of Edward Senay to chapter 7.

Behind
the Wall of
Respect

Behind the Wall of Respect

1

It was behind the Wall of Respect that Noel Barker, Gail Crawford, and I first penetrated Chicago's heroin subculture. It was behind these walls during the fall of 1968 that we were able to observe the dealing, the shooting up, the nodding,[1] the hustling, and the violence that were all part of that life. To artists and civil rights activists, 43d Street and Langley Avenue on Chicago's South Side was renowned for its brilliantly colored murals depicting rising pride and militancy among America's black and poor. But to Chicago's black addicts it was famous for another reason—it was one of the city's oldest "copping areas," a street corner where heroin had been sold almost continuously for the past twenty years.

With the help and protection of "Rabbi," a long-time heroin dealer recently turned methadone patient, we began our careful epidemiological observations of active addicts in their natural setting to determine how medical treatment systems might eventually eradicate such places altogether. Through informal observations, interviews, and visits to their homes, we eventually discovered the pharmacological principles underlying the unique social and geographical organization of this heroin copping area and others like it in Chicago and other

3

American cities. It was in the bars, pool halls, and abandoned buildings at 43d and Langley that we first developed a treatment outreach project to involve twenty-six active street addicts in methadone programs; the eventual goal was the total elimination of active heroin addiction in such communities.

While our initial intervention project did not eliminate addiction at 43d Street, it did permit us to develop operational field concepts and techniques for monitoring the number of active heroin addicts before, during, and after intervention projects. And it did permit us to experiment with treatment-oriented, nonpunitive strategies for neighborhood level addiction control.

Later we developed projects in other Chicago neighborhoods and found that black, white, and Spanish-speaking addicts all shared similar patterns of social and geographical organization, and could be contacted by outreach workers at local heroin distribution sites. In these community projects we improved our intervention techniques and were able to remove three-fourths of the active street addicts selected for intensive treatment outreach. But our model was still deficient: six months later the number of active addicts at target copping areas had returned to pre-intervention levels. And our model at this stage did not permit us to monitor or intervene in the massive heroin epidemic that struck Chicago and other American cities in the late 1960s.

To alter the course of a heroin epidemic, we required an entirely new set of field concepts and intervention techniques; so we returned to the field to observe new young addicts in epidemic neighborhoods. We attempted to document the process by which heroin spread, again looking for clues to a treatment-oriented intervention strategy. Our studies on the interpersonal routes of heroin spread and on the association patterns of the young addicts suggested an intervention approach analogous to that used to prevent spread of venereal disease. Projects based upon these public health principles were then initiated in two communities. One was a middle-class white neighborhood, where we successfully demonstrated the feasibility of an early identification and treatment outreach response to contain heroin spread. The other was our most ambitious project to date: the establishment of a comprehensive treatment program in an epidemic neighborhood with active community involvement and persistent epidemiological outreach. The neighborhood chosen was Altgeld Gardens, a black public housing project with a serious heroin epidemic among its young people.

The people and events that proved crucial to the success of these community addiction control experiments provide the substance of our story. It is the story of how physicians, social scientists, and ex-drug users worked together to design treatment programs to reduce dramatically the number of chronic addicts in the community and to prevent additional young people from joining future generations of addicts.

But because these community projects addressed such fundamental questions regarding the epidemiology of heroin addiction and the design of community addiction control programs, they might have been conducted at some other point in time. So we must ask, why 1968 and why Chicago?

Why 1968?

In partial answer, we can say that these programs were a product of a unique period in American history—the mid 1960s, an era of great optimism that technocratic solutions could be found for our society's most difficult urban problems. The projects to be described incorporated many of the themes of that period: they were neighborhood based with community involvement, and they recruited indigenous leaders, in this case the addict himself, as program staff. The professionals involved in these projects were also a part of that period. They shared a deep philosophical concern for the problems of American cities and their disadvantaged minorities, and hoped to strengthen the social and economic structure of these communities. We must recall that in the mid-1960s narcotic addiction in America was seen as a problem of the urban ghetto, primarily affecting the poor, the black, and the Spanish speaking.

The community mental health emphasis on locating programs in the community and on recruiting ex-addicts and local residents as staff and as members of advisory boards permitted physicians and epidemiologists a perspective on the drug problem not possible during the 1930s, 1940s, and 1950s when treatment and research were concentrated in large institutions, at considerable distance from the addict's natural setting. No longer outsiders to the communities that breed addiction, physicians and epidemiologists now had legitimate access to the homes, families, and meeting places of their drug-using patients. This direct interaction with the addict's natural setting and with ex-addicts and community residents largely eliminated the narrower perspectives of previous generations of professionals. Research and planning became more relevant and less theoretical.

Our community addiction control experiments were also made possible by significant advances in treatment technology. The early 1960s saw decades of pessimism shattered when a small group of ex-addicts in southern California, living in a therapeutic community called Synanon,[2] began to claim spectacular cures. Their approach was to place forty or more addicts in a large home or small camp under the supervision of ex–drug users who were highly skilled in group techniques. From the time of his admission the addict was required to act in a responsible and mature manner. His behavior was under continuous surveillance, and conformity to the rules of the community was reinforced by a system of rewards and enhanced social status. If an addict broke a serious rule, he was punished by assignment to a low-status job or even humiliated by having his head shaved and being required to carry a sign to advertise his "stupidity." Frustrations were worked through in intense encounter groups. Synanon staff members served as role models for the new resident. Because they were ex-addicts themselves, they knew the ins and outs of addict behavior and could not be manipulated the way professionally trained therapists often were. Their interaction with the addict was the crucial ingredient in Synanon's success.

By the mid-1960s this therapeutic dynamic had been reproduced at Daytop Village in New York City,[3] and by Dr. Efren Ramirez in Puerto Rico.[4] It was now possible to think of setting up a large number of therapeutic communities, should this be desirable. But to resocialize most drug abusers approximately two years in a therapeutic community were required, and at the start of our Chicago projects there were still no systematic data on their effectiveness in producing long-term changes in the drug addict. Although therapeutic communities were beginning to produce significant numbers of impressive graduates, they accepted only

motivated individuals and even many of these dropped out before
completing treatment.[5] In addition, there was the problem of the
high cost of maintaining an individual in 24-hour residence for a
period of two years.[6]

A second breakthrough in treatment technology was methadone maintenance. Methadone is a synthetic narcotic drug,
which when taken by mouth has a duration of action of approximately 24 hours. When it is dispensed in a clinic, the addict finds
it necessary to report only once daily to avoid withdrawal
symptoms. Intake of the drug can be observed so that the
problem of diversion of narcotics to the street is minimized. If an
addict were maintained on intravenous heroin or morphine, he
would be required to report three or more times a day for
observed injection, because of the shorter duration of action of
these drugs, particularly when taken intravenously. Methadone
has other advantages: when taken by mouth it generally produces
less euphoria than injected heroin, and if a methadone-maintained addict injects the usual quantities of heroin he is unlikely
to experience any euphoria at all. Unless large amounts are
injected—which is expensive—the heroin is not a rewarding
experience.

There are problems with methadone maintenance. If an addict
stops reporting to the clinic, he will experience a severe narcotic
withdrawal syndrome similar to that of heroin addiction and will
be required to use heroin or other opiates for relief. Methadone is
thus not a cure; it actually perpetuates addiction. In effect the
methadone patient is as dependent upon the clinic as he was
formerly dependent upon the drug dealer. But methadone does
permit the addict to stabilize his life situation. Because the
treatment is usually free of charge, he is not forced to raise $50 or
more per day for illegal heroin of unknown purity and strength.
Many methadone clinics have counselors to assist the addict in
finding a job or education, and to help him with his adjustment
problems. At the time we initiated our Chicago research,
Drs. Vincent Dole and Marie Nyswander were reporting that 87%
of chronic addicts assigned to methadone maintenance remained
in treatment and 70% of these were either working or in some
form of training.[7] Despite these encouraging results and the low
cost of this treatment,[8] it was observed that most patients had

difficulty withdrawing from methadone after they had rein-
tegrated into society. It was not yet clear what proportion of
patients must continue the treatment for long periods. [9]

In addition to methadone, other pharmacotherapies were being
tested. The most promising of these was L-alpha-acetylmethadol,
often referred to as LAAM. [10] This is a methadone-like synthetic
opiate which has a 72-hour duration of action. It has the
advantage that the addict must report for his medication only
once every three days, thereby increasing his willingness to
cooperate in treatment.

Several other drugs referred to as "narcotic antagonists" are
also being explored. Cyclazocine has been most extensively
researched, but many patients experience undesirable side effects. Naltrexone has recently undergone clinical trials with few
side effects and seems to show considerable promise. [11] If an
individual takes cyclazocine or naltrexone regularly and then
injects heroin or any other opiate, he will not experience euphoria. These drugs are called narcotic antagonists because they
are believed to compete with the opiate molecule for the same
neuroreceptor sites. When they are present in sufficient quantities, they block the usual euphoric effect of the opiate molecules. They can also produce an acute withdrawal syndrome in
active heroin addicts, presumably due to a sudden replacement of
opiate molecules by antagonist molecules at the receptor sites. [12]
The disadvantage of this agent is that an addict can stop taking
the blocking agent at any time and in several days he can enjoy
the full euphoria of heroin.

Why Chicago?

Compared to California and New York, the state of Illinois was a
latecomer to the field of drug addiction treatment. However, this
had its advantages because Illinois benefited from the experiences of the other states, and by the late 1960s there were
promising treatment approaches available. Still, there had not yet
been a clear analysis of the relative cost and effectiveness of these
treatments. While some evaluation data were available, comparisons between different approaches were difficult because the
treatments were delivered in different types of institutional

settings; evaluation criteria and sample selection methods were rarely comparable.

The Illinois Drug Abuse Program (IDAP) developed at a time when it was possible to think of organizing the various treatment approaches or modalities under a single administration and then comparing their relative cost and effectiveness; IDAP thus pioneered the idea of the "multimodality" treatment program. The program had still another unique advantage in that Chicago did not have the pressing drug problem of New York City. It was possible to think in terms of a carefully evaluated pilot treatment program before expanding into a statewide system.

With the appointment of Dr. Jerome Jaffe as director, the treatment system came under the management of a psychiatrist with considerable experience in drug dependence research. Because of the need for research expertise, the program became a joint effort of the University of Chicago Department of Psychiatry and the State of Illinois Department of Mental Health. During the early phase of IDAP, then, each treatment facility was viewed as an experimental program. This experimental orientation to the problem of treatment led not only to systematic comparisons of established approaches but also to innovation and evaluation of new approaches.[13] The program concept was ideal for launching our community treatment programs. IDAP was dynamic and experimental, not rigid or bureaucratic, and it served Chicago, America's second largest city with the full range of drug and community problems.

When I arrived in Chicago in July 1968 I found the embryo of what was to become IDAP. There was one small inpatient unit at the University of Chicago Hospital, and one outpatient methadone clinic a block away. That month we started our first patient on cyclazocine. While I looked for a place to live I stayed at Gateway House, a beautiful mansion in Chicago's South Shore neighborhood and the midwest's first therapeutic community for drug addicts.

Before I could start my study of Chicago's street addicts, I served for several months as clinical director of IDAP until a suitable person could be recruited for the job. It was an exciting period in the development of this historic treatment program. During this period we developed the basic staff structure of

IDAP, which was to become a pacesetter in its use of ex-addict personnel for virtually all treatment roles other than those filled by physicians and nurses.[14] It was a good time to be clinical director because I worked closely with the people who eventually occupied key roles in this statewide treatment system, which in a few years grew to fifty community facilities with over 5,000 addicts in treatment.

The core of the IDAP program was the methadone outpatient clinic. A typical clinic served about 100 patients and was staffed by a part-time physician, two nurses, and an ex-addict counselor for every twenty patients. The patient's progress was monitored by three urine tests each week to check on his use of illicit drugs. The patient and his counselor also completed a weekly report on his progress in treatment and employment, and on contacts with the police. During any week each patient had one or more individual contacts with his counselor and the majority of patients attended at least one group counseling session. The patient was assigned to a clinic as near to his residence as possible. He rarely found himself in a strange environment; he invariably knew other patients in the clinic and frequently some of the ex-addict staff as well. A clinic in a black neighborhood was generally served by black staff. If patients were predominantly Latin or white, the staff also tended to be Latin or white. In treatment facilities the atmosphere was generally warm and informal, which is in part due to the sociable nature of addicts when they come together, and in part due to the successful working of a therapeutic milieu.

When the IDAP treatment system was fully developed in 1971, approximately 81% of the patients were in methadone clinics, 11% were residents of therapeutic communities, 4% were residential methadone patients, and 4% were abstinent outpatients.[15]

Our Goal:
Neighborhood Level Addiction Control

It was clear from the start that IDAP would help many addicts to rejoin society as productive citizens, but would it also serve as an instrument of addiction control? Would there be fewer addicts on the streets of Chicago as a result of these treatment programs, or would dealers simply recruit new addicts to replace those that were treated? Would IDAP appeal only to the most motivated, leaving the majority of addicts in the community unaffected? My colleagues and I, in forming our epidemiology unit, assigned ourselves the responsibility to design treatment programs that would reach the vast majority of addicts in the community and to make this treatment system an effective, nonpunitive, instrument of addiction control.

On the surface our task was simple: find a high drug-use neighborhood, count the number of addicts, set up a multi-modality treatment program, and then count the number of addicts again. To the extent that there were fewer active addicts in the neighborhood, our program could claim success.

But how does one count active drug addicts? We were familiar with some excellent work on this question in small towns in England.[16] But British addicts during the mid-1960s obtained most of their heroin from physicians, so that British epidemiologists did not have the highly criminalized addict subculture to consider in conducting their studies. In addition, we were starting in a large urban area, not in a small circumscribed community. Our initial problem, then, was how to gain access to the addict subculture in one of Chicago's high drug-use neighborhoods.

Developing a Mobile
Epidemiological Team

2

Social scientists had developed techniques to study heroin addicts in their natural setting, but their research generally addressed theoretical issues more of concern to other social scientists than to treatment program planners.[1] Our needs were more general. We too would be conducting specific research studies using interview and questionnaire survey techniques, and we would also collect data through the participant observer approach, but our ultimate goal was to develop an intervention function. In effect, we were establishing a new role with multiple functions, a role that would carry a drug treatment system's presence into the addict's natural setting. This presence could not be limited to a particular group of addicts in one or two neighborhoods. We needed a mobile epidemiological team with access to the active addicts of any Chicago neighborhood.

But gaining access to active addicts is not a simple matter in American communities. They keep their activities secret and are suspicious of anyone seeking information about these activities—with good reason, because narcotic

Portions of this chapter appeared originally in P. H. Hughes, G. A. Crawford, and N. W. Barker, "Developing an Epidemiologic Field Team for Drug Dependence," *Archives of General Psychiatry* 24, no. 5 (1971): 389–93.

enforcement agencies routinely use informers and undercover agents to set up addicts for arrest. The addict can't afford to answer truthfully such simple questions as, "What is your name?" or, "Where do you live?" Even an addict's close friends often know him only by his street name, and just as often they do not know where he lives. Thus we would face considerable difficulty in obtaining accurate information and perhaps even greater difficulty in checking its accuracy.

Because heroin traffic is linked with organized crime, working with addicts in their natural setting is more dangerous than working with street gangs. A street-gang worker can usually get to know the gang leaders; there is no hierarchy above his working contacts to pose a threat. Among addicts, on the other hand, there are always individuals in the drug distribution hierarchy who are suspicious of anyone with information that could lead to their arrest. Because violence is an inherent part of the addict street scene in contemporary America, we were concerned about exposing ourselves and our field-workers to personal danger.

Exploring Field-Worker Models

Not knowing quite where to start, we reviewed a variety of fieldwork roles that had already been established for performing similar functions. None, however, seemed perfectly suited to our needs. The field research roles of the social scientist had to do with data collection, but included no intervention functions. We found the general approach of the street-gang worker[2] was also relevant—making contact with gang leaders and redirecting them into productive alternative activities—but with addicts this strategy would not be feasible. Much as the addicts on the corner might wish to play baseball or organize a community car wash, their addiction did not permit it: they were constantly on the go, hustling for drugs.

We examined the police officer's role in obtaining information about addicts and initiating intervention procedures. The Chicago Police Department had a "fieldwork" force of 12,000 officers[3] with extensive knowledge of drug addiction in every neighborhood. We talked to narcotics officers about how they obtained information on addicts in the community, that is, through informers, undercover agents, and beat patrolmen, and we were particularly impressed with how they protected the identity of their informers and how they used their power base—the ability to arrest or not arrest—as a lever for obtaining information.[4] Much to our relief, they indicated that our field-workers would not be effective if they were identified with the police. They respected the need for confidentiality of treatment program information and assured us they would not attempt to obtain our fieldwork data for law enforcement purposes.

Our most productive visit was to the Venereal Disease Control Unit at the Chicago Board of Health. This unit, the epidemiological data gathering center and the major prevention and control arm of the venereal disease treatment system, had the very functions that we were proposing for our field team. We found the activities of the venereal disease investigator (VDI) to be based on a thorough epidemiological analysis of the dynamics of syphilis and gonorrhea communicability.[5] When new cases are uncovered they are interviewed by the VDI to locate sexual contacts during the communicable stage of the disorder. These contacts are in turn approached for blood tests, smears, and treatment. Because it had mobile epidemiological teams, the unit was able to identify new disease outbreaks at an early stage and to launch a treatment response quickly to prevent the outbreak from spreading further. The unit even had case-finding forms for organizing the VDI's activities in containing new outbreaks; we found these useful in later stages of our work. The VDI also had to deal with some of the same problems of confidentiality which confronted us, since individuals with venereal disease were often reluctant to identify their sexual contacts and were fearful of exposing themselves. We were even dealing with some of the same people—the investigators we interviewed found addict prostitutes among their most active disease spreaders.

Early Field-Workers and Early Problems

When I first arrived in Chicago and began looking for ex-addicts to become potential members of our epidemiological team, I met Clyde Johnson,[6] who was then a counselor in IDAP's first methadone clinic. Most staff members considered Clyde to be well informed on the local addict street scene, so we drove together to a number of addict street hangouts in black neighborhoods of Chicago's South Side. He would not take me into the bars and pool halls in these areas because he considered them too dangerous for me, but some of the addicts would come over to the car and talk to Clyde about how they were doing and ask about the treatment program. I felt good; the street addict meeting places in Chicago were very much like those I had observed in New York.

I started to build our team; we held meetings each week even though I was very busy with clinical work and the development of new treatment facilities. The first meetings included Clyde, several addict patients from his clinic, and Noel Barker, a sociology graduate student from the University of Chicago. During exploratory discussions we developed a map of heroin addict hangouts on the South Side and began to think through the plans for the coming year.

In the early fall of 1968 I was given the go-ahead to hire one field-worker. I had not yet found the right person, so I split the funds to cover three part-time jobs and I hired Clyde, Willie George, and Eugene Allen. All three were black and in their thirties or forties. Willie was a very quiet, likable fellow who at that time worked as a mailman; he was recommended because he had good contacts with addicts on the far South Side, where he and his brothers ran the neighborhood numbers racket. Eugene was hired because he was a well-known entertainer in Chicago's black nightclubs; he was liked and had high social status among addicts. We picked up a fourth field-worker when Gary Washington, also a black, was assigned to our unit full-time by IDAP. Gary had had trouble on his other job in the program, but no one wanted to fire him and the administration "thought maybe you could use him."[7] About this time Gail Crawford, then a sociology graduate student from the University of Illinois, joined our team, and IDAP recruited a clinical director, which freed me to devote most of my time to the epidemiology project.

Our first task was to develop case-finding procedures to identify all active addicts in high drug-use neighborhoods. Our initial approach was simply to ask the field-workers to estimate the number of addicts who met at the hangouts in each of their neighborhoods. This was not very useful; they gave estimates ranging from 200 to 2,000 for the same neighborhoods. Next we asked them to bring us names of all the addicts they knew in their respective neighborhoods; this did not work either. They brought us incomplete lists written on scraps of paper, with names like "Foots" and "Sharkie"—few real names, mostly aliases or street names.

We quickly saw the need for a questionnaire which would make possible systematic data collection, but we knew it would not be realistic to give our field-workers long forms to take into the community for completion on the street corner. Earlier, we had been impressed with the handy 3 x 5-inch addict case-reporting slips used by the Federal Bureau of Narcotics to obtain data for national drug arrest statistics. We decided to design a similar card for collecting basic epidemiological data on addicts in the community. The 5 x 9-inch green case-finding card which resulted could be folded and carried in the field worker's pocket, making it convenient for use on the street. Our green card turned out to be a real breakthrough for the project because it gave us information on where the addict lived, his age, and the drugs he used; some of the questions were identical to those on the Federal Bureau of Narcotics form, permitting comparisons of our data with Chicago arrest data.

Our greatest weakness at this point, though, was our field-workers. This can be illustrated by describing a field visit I made one afternoon with Gary to an addict hangout on 63d Street. As we entered a large pool hall, I thought to myself that I had never seen so many hip-looking addicts and hustlers in my life—there must have been seventy-five—most of them leaning against the walls and a few were nodding. Above the shoeshine stand hung an amusing sign: "No Loafing, No Addicts, No Pushers." This was the place. Gary said hello to a few of the people he knew, and within minutes several pool tables were transformed into desks, with the majority of the men in the room filling out our green cards. I was talking with two of my methadone patients who happened to be there when suddenly all eyes turned to the door. A beat patrolman was making his rounds. Neither Gary nor I were happy to see him. Here we had addicts writing down their names and addresses and it looked as if a policeman was coming in to gather up the cards. Fortunately the officer was a very reasonable man who was as amused by the situation as we were uncomfortable. He simply asked a few questions about what was going on, and when Gary told him we were trying to help the addicts get on the treatment program, he said that sounded good to him and he left—to our great relief.

But if I was nervous in this situation, Gary was petrified. We soon learned that he was spending very little time at addict hangouts in his neighborhood. He would visit, talk to some people, have a few cards filled out, and leave. Gary was afraid. For one thing, he was trying to get away from the street scene. He wasn't receiving methadone, so when he visited the street he felt exposed to the temptation of slipping back into the habit. Gary also feared what the dealers thought about his activities on 63d Street. Initially he had presented himself to us as a big man on the street, and in fact he did have a good reputation as a gambler and con artist. But even though Gary and our other field-workers were liked and highly respected among addicts in these neighborhoods, they were themselves in awe of "the Man"—the drug dealer.[8] The addict's life centers around his relationship with the Man: if he can't find him he gets terribly sick; if he doesn't have money, he has literally to beg for drugs. But, most important, the addict has learned over time that the Man is violent. He has to be violent or addicts will simply take away his drugs. He must be feared or informers will not hesitate to set him up for arrest. All our field-workers had seen how the Man dealt with informers or anyone else who threatened his operations. The Man invariably carried a pistol or at least a knife, and he usually operated with a partner. Most dealers were backed up by the "main people," those higher up in the drug distribution system. The Man was not somebody to mess with.

The field team we had initially been so pleased to have pulled together was, after a few weeks, on the verge of disintegration. Willie lost his post office job and began slipping back into heroin use. Eugene was suddenly hospitalized for surgery. Gary and Clyde, increasingly anxious about exposing themselves to the temptations and dangers of the street, began to hide their anxiety by reinforcing one another in resisting what Gail, Noel, and I asked them to do. At the height of these difficulties, Clyde suggested that if Noel and I wanted to visit addict hangouts we should put on turtleneck sweaters and sport coats—the kind narcotic detectives typically wear—and go into the bars and pool halls by ourselves. Everyone would think we were police, he said, so they wouldn't bother us. I was very discouraged and began to question our concept of the ex-addict field-worker.

Hiring the Man

When Willie relapsed into heroin use we had to let him go; this freed one of our part-time positions and I began looking for a replacement. Sonny Koretsky, who was then directing the 79th Street clinic, told me about Rabbi. Here was a man, Sonny said, who was really cool, who carried a lot of weight with local addicts. He said he would have hired Rabbi as a counselor trainee on his own staff, but he had no openings. Sonny was a little, white, Jewish ex-addict who was trained at Daytop Village in New York. Here he was on the South Side of Chicago, managing a large clinic for black addicts. Putting 100 addicts into a clinic and trying to get them to act like Sunday school boys was no easy task. Some of his early patients had threatened to beat up the nurse when she refused to give them extra methadone, so his counselors were all big, black ex-addicts with a reputation for violence. When addicts came into the 79th Street clinic now, they acted like gentlemen—and ladies. When Matt Rice, one of Sonny's group therapy counselors, said "group therapy time," the patients grouped.

Sonny had sent us a good man. Rabbi had for many years been the major heroin dealer at 43d Street and Langley Avenue. He was about six foot three and had a ragged scar running from his right cheek down across both lips. Like many big men he smiled a lot and was very easygoing. Even though he was in his mid-forties he was strong and athletic looking.

We hired Rabbi on the spot. He said it would take him a few days to arrange for us to visit the hangouts in his neighborhood. That same week Noel and I made our first visit to the Wall of Respect, which was deep in the black ghetto. It would be dangerous for whites to go there alone, but with Rabbi we had no anxiety. The following week Gail went with him, and thereafter we made regular visits to the area. We found the addicts were not suspicious or afraid to talk to us; in fact, they seemed eager to see the doctor and the sociologists who wanted to help them get into the treatment program. It was not necessary to look for the addicts; they came to us. Rabbi had told the bartenders, the pool hall owners, and the dealers that we would be coming, so everything was cool. He began to distribute the green cards.

As excited as we were about the breakthrough Rabbi was making on 43d Street, much of what we saw was very sad. On our first visit we were approached by Bird Dog, a middle-aged overweight addict who showed us ugly festering ulcers on his leg which had been caused by injecting paregoric. We met a young prostitute, very thin and with a bad cough. Another addict had two cases (arrests) on him, so the dealers were afraid to sell to him as he might be under pressure to inform. All were desperate to enter the treatment program.

Most of the action at 43d and Langley took place in two bars and a pool hall. One of the bars was in the building with the beautiful murals, on the southeast corner. In the other bar across the street, Rabbi's wife worked as a waitress. On the southwest corner was the abandoned building with murals where addicts would go to shoot up; those who had no place to stay would sleep in the empty apartments. A few years later this building was pulled down, but a part of the wall with the murals was moved to Malcolm X College, where it is now on permanent display.

Could the Team Collect Meaningful Data?

All our efforts to gain access to the street would be meaningless if we could not obtain systematic epidemiological data.[9] Our ex-addict field team would have to demonstrate its ability to perform a variety of epidemiological functions related to program planning, intensive case-finding, and intervention activity.

Program Planning

An issue of growing concern to the IDAP administration was that our patients were older than addicts seen in most other urban areas. Was the program attracting only older, "burned-out" addicts? Did it hold little attraction for younger addicts? How representative were IDAP patients of the total addict population on Chicago's South Side?

Using data obtained from survey cards collected in four different neighborhoods, we attempted to answer these questions. We compared characteristics of these addict street samples with IDAP treatment applicants and with 100 randomly chosen Chicago police arrestees from these same neighborhoods and found that our patients did appear to be representative of the addict population of these communities (see table 1). We did not find large numbers of new addicts on the streets at that time, suggesting that the older age of addicts seeking treatment actually reflected the older age of addicts in the community. From these data IDAP administration was reassured that the program was not restricting itself to a small segment of the addict population on the South Side.

Table 1   Comparison of Three Samples of Black Addicts from Chicago's South Side

Data	Street Sample	Treatment Program Sample	BNDD Arrest Sample[a]
% Negro (N)	100 (149)	100 (196)[b]	100 (100)
Mean age in years (N)	36.5 (141)	36.2 (196)[b]	37.5 (100)
Mean years since first heroin use (N)	15.9 (149)	13.8 (298)[c]	9.0 (100)

[a] 100 addicts were randomly picked from police arrestees in these communities.
[b] These data were obtained from a larger sample of 845 patients who had completed intake.
[c] This figure was obtained from an earlier analysis of 298 Drug Abuse Program patients, 71.3% of whom are black.

Another planning question that concerned us was whether the incidence of new cases in our target communities was increasing or decreasing.[10] For this analysis we plotted the self-reported year of first heroin use for our street survey sample and for a patient sample from these same communities. We found the incidence of initial heroin use in this target population had been extremely low during the preceding fifteen years when compared with the period from 1946 to 1950 (see fig. 1). This suggested that the challenge facing IDAP in these communities was the rehabilitation of middle-aged addicts, most of whom had become addicted some twenty years before in what appeared to have been a serious heroin "epidemic." Although the incidence of first heroin use had been relatively low in recent years, we saw a disturbing increase in initial heroin use trends during the preceding three years, 1965–68. We were concerned about this disturbing upswing but were not yet aware we were observing an early sign of America's massive heroin epidemic of the late 1960s.

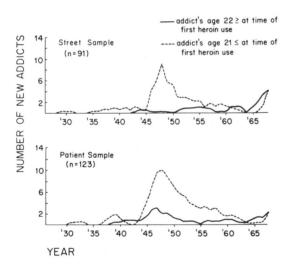

Fig. 1.   Year of first heroin use trends in two samples of black addicts

The IDAP planners also wanted to know how accurately the Federal Bureau of Narcotics (FBN)[11] case registry data reflected the total number of addicts in Chicago and Illinois. We found the FBN case-finding data to be nearly complete: 73% of our initial street sample of 113 addicts were known to the FBN under the name given on our survey cards.[12] Because arrest data are often recorded under the narcotic user's alias, it is likely that the percentage of these middle-aged chronic addicts known to the bureau was actually higher than 73.

Intensive Case-finding

Thinking ahead to our future projects, we wished to know if we could obtain systematic data on all the active addicts in neighborhoods selected for intervention projects. To answer this question we asked Rabbi to administer green cards to all addicts in his neighborhood. Of 49 addicts he knew to be regular visitors to 43d Street during the month of January 1969, 26 completed the cards. Some remained suspicious, and it was not until June that he obtained cards from 63 (87.5%) of the 72 addicts who had been regular visitors during the six-month period.[13] For 39 of these 63 addicts there were no applications for treatment on file in the IDAP Admission Unit; without an epidemiological team they would not otherwise have been known to the treatment program at this time.

Intervention Activity

By late 1968 we were still not clear how the field-worker was to perform intervention functions. We had earlier discarded the street-gang worker strategy of redirecting delinquents from criminal to socially approved activities. This approach had actually been tried earlier on heroin addicts in New York City by the Mobilization for Youth,[14] but had failed. A club had been formed, but it was difficult to get the addicts to attend meetings, and when the treasurer ran off with the club funds the effort was disbanded.

Because of the heroin addict's overriding preoccupation with the need to obtain drugs to avoid withdrawal symptoms, for an intervention to be truly effective it must first manage the pharmacological aspects of the condition through medical treatment. To determine if our field team could involve active addicts in treatment, we selected from Rabbi's neighborhood twenty-eight addicts who had not independently sought admission to IDAP. We found that sixteen or 58% could be involved in treatment simply by having Rabbi offer them direct admission to the program. Actually, the response might have been much better had the individuals in this particular project not been required to participate in a home visit and a questionnaire study prior to their admission. We must also bear in mind that they presumably numbered among the more resistant addicts because they had not sought treatment on their own.

Rabbi on 43d Street

The Wall of Respect at 43d Street and Langley
Avenue, Chicago (Ebony Magazine photograph)

Typical Chicago copping area

Intravenous injection of heroin:
(a) mixing white heroin powder and water in bottle cap
(b) cooking up
(c) filling syringe
(d) shooting up

(b)

(d)

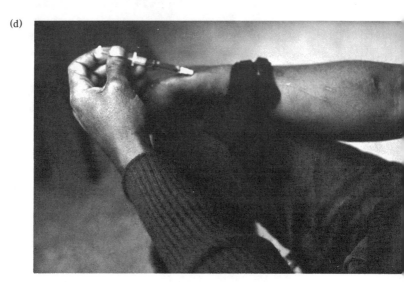

Spellman Young at Day One Clinic.

Dick Parker, ethnographer, checked by Chicago
police during field visit

Checking Reliability

In any form of research it is necessary to establish the reliability of the data. This was even more important in our work because our field-workers were ex-addicts who by definition had low credibility. The reliability of two types of data would have to be checked: the field reports of our team, and information which the addicts themselves wrote down on the green cards and questionnaires.

To check Rabbi's observational data—which he recorded each week in a logbook—Noel, Gail, and I during our visits to 43d Street made independent observations, questioning addicts we met on material covered in Rabbi's reports. In this way we were able to determine the correspondence of Rabbi's reports with our own data. Generally we found a high level of agreement. Where there were differences, they tended to be minor; for example, was Tom Jackson arrested two or four weeks ago?

To check the reliability of data on the green cards and questionnaires, we examined the responses of the same individuals to identical questions on IDAP admission questionnaires when they entered treatment. Here again, we were encouraged to find a great deal of correspondence in the two sets of data. Differences appeared to be due to limitations of memory and recall rather than to deliberate distortion. In later field projects we adopted these same procedures to check the reliability of data.

A Functioning Field Team

In recruiting ex-addicts for our fieldwork role, we encountered two major problems: the first was the field-workers' fear of being seen as police informers. This problem was resolved when we chose a high-status, trusted ex-drug dealer as a field-worker, a principle we followed in subsequent recruitment. The ex-drug dealer has intimate experience in the workings of the addict social system; he knows its rules and how it is maintained.

A second major problem faced by the field-workers was the temptation of continual exposure to drugs on the street; some were not able to handle this. We subsequently resolved this problem by recruiting either methadone-maintained ex-addicts or IDAP counselors. Methadone patients did not risk relapse even if they tried heroin once or twice. We found IDAP counselors were also able to visit the street with little danger, as they appeared to be protected by the continuous support and reinforcement they received from their jobs.

Our original anxieties about obtaining cooperation from street addicts proved groundless. Because we were attached to a voluntary treatment system, they saw us as having legitimate reasons for being in their community. In fact, many even welcomed us because they were in desperate need of treatment and saw us as a source of help. We found ourselves in an excellent position to receive data in return for treatment help. Even our early concern over our personal safety disappeared when we learned that many of the addicted dealers saw us as a potential source of help for themselves at some time in the future. The other dealers were not threatened because they had more business than they could handle. Of fundamental importance in all this was everyone's understanding that we would give no information to the police. The IDAP had already gained the confidence of addicts in the community that information would be used for treatment purposes only, never to arrest drug users or dealers. We benefited from IDAP's good reputation and from the principle of medical confidentiality.

Even though we now had a field team which could give us access to active addicts in the community, and could even bring them into treatment, we had not yet developed functional concepts for looking at the street addict population in an organized way. We needed operational field concepts which would locate addicts as members of a definable social system rather than as individual social units. To develop these concepts, we looked deeper into the dynamics of Chicago's heroin addict subculture.

Penetrating Chicago's Heroin Subculture

3 It was the fashion, when we began our studies, for professionals in the drug abuse field to speak glibly about the "addict subculture." This was due in large part to the emergence of the ex-addict as a key member of the contemporary treatment team. Because he knew the rules of the subculture, the ex-addict was often in a better position than professionally trained staff to "manipulate" addict patients in the rehabilitation process.

I had come to appreciate the importance of understanding the addict subculture several years earlier at the Fort Worth, Texas, Federal Narcotics Hospital, where I had found it necessary to study the dynamics of the addict prisoner community before I could design an effective rehabilitation process.[1] To me it seemed only natural to repeat this same strategy in Chicago. First we would conduct a thorough analysis of the heroin subculture on the neighborhood level; then, based upon the dynamics observed, we would design realistic programs.

Portions of this chapter appeared originally in P. H. Hughes and J. H. Jaffe, "The Heroin Copping Area: A Location for Epidemiological Study and Intervention Activity," *Archives of General Psychiatry* 24, no. 5 (1971): 394–400, and in P. H. Hughes, G. A. Crawford, N. W. Barker, S. Schumann, and J. H. Jaffe, "The Social Structure of a Heroin Copping Community," *American Journal of Psychiatry* 128, no. 5 (1971): 551–58. © 1971 the American Psychiatric Association.

Heroin Subculture Studies

Fortunately our effort to understand Chicago's heroin subculture
was able to draw upon a number of earlier studies. The most vivid
subcultural descriptions, of course, are those of journalists and
novelists. For example, *The Addict in the Street,* by Larner and
Tefferteller,[2] presents a series of interviews with young New York
City addicts to give highly personalized accounts of their lives as
addicts, their introduction to drug use, their changing relations
with family, and their frightening experiences with police, drug
overdose, and violence. One of the most graphic descriptions in
the literature is *The Panic in Needle Park,* by James Mills,[3] a
newsreporter's account of a sudden heroin shortage in New York
City in 1964. Mills follows two addicts, Bob and Helen, through
this crisis period, taking the reader to meet their addict ac-
quaintances and to visit some of the city's addict meeting places,
such as 47th Street at 7th Avenue and 82d Street at Columbus
Avenue.

One of the earliest and most perceptive sociological studies of
the addict subculture was conducted by Harold Finestone at the
University of Chicago during the early 1950s.[4] In describing the
social dynamics of Chicago's young black heroin addicts, he
introduced the concept of the "cool cat"—the black youth who
rejected the menial jobs, drudgery, and humiliation that were his
traditional lot in America. The cat was proud, not subservient—
choosing easy money over an honest job, choosing to use his
charm and his wits rather than his hands and his back, choosing
stylish and colorful garb over drab work clothes, choosing to
exploit women rather than marry and raise a family in poverty.
Through a harmonious combination of charm, language, un-
restrained generosity, and drug use, the cat felt himself any
man's equal, and infinitely superior to the "squares" who
accepted the black man's traditional status and identity. Finestone's description of the unique characteristics of this subculture
and his analysis of its socioeconomic origins provided a historic
starting point for later students.

Some students of deviance theory have found it convenient to
view drug users as belonging to a retreatist subculture. In fact,
Richard Cloward[5] had labeled the addict as belonging to a culture

of double failures: unable to compete successfully in both legitimate and illegitimate opportunity systems, the double failure escapes with others like himself into a society of drug users. But recently this theoretical notion of addicts belonging to a retreatist subculture has been challenged by empirical study. Alan Sutter's[6] interviews of San Francisco drug users revealed a variety of social types that were neither passive nor retreatist. The subculture he described had an elaborate status system based upon the type of drug used and the type of illegal occupation or hustle, and upon conformity to subcultural norms, such as the prohibition against informing. At the very top of this status hierarchy he found the "righteous dope fiend"—the successful addict—rarely seen in hospitals or prisons who, while fully addicted to heroin, actively pursued and achieved a wide variety of illegitimate success goals.

Harvey Feldman also challenges the concept of the retreatist and passive addict subculture.[7] Employing participant observer techniques in a Boston neighborhood, he found drug use as just one of many daring and risky behaviors required for high status in the community's "hip" street society. He suggested that drugs might not be used for their psychopharmacological effects as much as to show manhood by engaging in a dangerous activity. Heroin use thus brought the highest social ranking, while marijuana use, because of its less damaging health and legal effects, conferred less status.

Two other studies are noteworthy for their systematic descriptions and for the unique research approaches employed. In *Ripping and Running,* Michael Agar[8] describes his attempt, as an ethnographer, to isolate the core activities shared by members of the heroin subculture. The rich and systematic data were collected, of all places, in the Lexington Federal Narcotics Hospital by enlisting addict prisoners to act out and to role play their daily experiences as former heroin users in the community. In reducing these core activities to hustling for money, copping the drug, and shooting up, he also showed the great variation in these activities caused by different environmental contingencies. In *Connections: Notes from the Heroin World,* Gould and his associates[9] offer a rich description of the heroin subculture of New Haven by reporting observations from three different perspec-

tives: narcotic police interaction with addicts, treatment personnel interaction with addicts, and participant observer interaction
with active heroin users in the community.

The preceding studies have greatly enriched our understanding
of the dynamics of the addict subculture, but they address
theoretical and methodological issues of primary concern to
social scientists. They largely ignore the issue of intervention
programs and control. Because our purpose was to count and
treat addicts, we required a more concrete and practical con-
ception of the addict subculture. For this reason, Preble and
Casey's description of the role structure of the heroin distribution
system proved more relevant to our needs.[10] By describing the
various stages and the participants from the time opium is grown
in the fields to the moment it reaches the consumer, they brought
a functional and quantitative definition to the previously mysteri-
ous heroin distribution system. Their description included the
types and numbers of people involved, the quantities and purity
of heroin, and the economics at the various stages.

Building upon these studies, then, and particularly the work of
Preble and Casey, we began our study of Chicago's heroin
subculture, searching for operational field research and intervention concepts. Our inquiry examined the social, the geographical, and the role dynamics of the addicts who gathered at 43d
Street, and in the end, each of these three separate frameworks
for study proved necessary building blocks for the intervention
projects that followed.

Social Dynamics

Much of our understanding of the social dynamics operating
within the addict subculture was acquired gradually and in-
formally during visits to the streets and during our work with
field-workers and patients. But when Rabbi first joined our team,
we found him to be such a rich source of insights and information that Noel, Gail, and I spent many afternoons in more formal
discussions with him to review areas that were unclear to us.

Codes

Chicago street addicts had codes similar to those I had observed
earlier among addicts in the institutional setting.[11] The funda-

mental code was, "Thou shall not inform to the police." Punishment for breaking this code varied according to the circumstances. If a violent and high-status individual was arrested on a serious charge and the informer was identified, he might be killed. The cleanest way was simply to give the informer a dose of pure or poisoned heroin; the police would be likely to view the victim as just another drug overdose and not as a homicide. The frequency of this type of punishment is difficult to determine, but it did occur once in Rabbi's copping area during the early phase of our studies. The addict in this case came to our office one day begging to be admitted to the treatment program, but he would give no reason for the urgency. Because his admission was part of a research study, we first had to involve him in interviews and a home visit, so we scheduled his workup to begin the following week. The next day we learned he had been found dead of a heroin overdose. Later, at the copping area, it was generally agreed that the man had been killed for informing.

The code against informing is more elaborate than a mere injunction not to give information to the police. It includes the notion of "taking one's own weight": if the police found three addicts together in a room with heroin or stolen property, one addict would assume guilt for the crime so that all three would not be charged. Usually the addict who had served the least time in jail, or had the least to lose if convicted, would "take the heat."

To our surprise, we found a seeming contradiction to the rules. As we came to know the addicts in Rabbi's community we learned that a number of the active heroin users we met were generally acknowledged to be informers. These people were relatively free from the fear of retaliation because they were very careful to "set up" heroin users who were either nonviolent or too weak to strike back; or they were so secretive in their dealings with police that no one could be sure they actually had informed.

Even though the code against informing was absolute, we found among addicts a general acceptance that a high percentage of their number would inform. The majority in Rabbi's neighborhood were middle-aged, chronic addicts with numerous arrests, they knew how a man's spirit could be broken after he had already spent many years in prison and then faced new charges that could result in another long sentence.[12]

Then there was another class of informers, some we had

actually met at the central narcotics unit of the Chicago police force. These informers enjoyed special police protection, and addicts in the community understood that, if these particular informers were killed, their neighborhoods would come under heavy police harrassment.

Sometimes the police have no charge to bring against a person they know to be an addict, but they pick him up simply to obtain information. Most addicts claim to have had this experience and say that, when this occurs, the officers threaten to lock them up for the night on a minor charge such as loitering or trespassing. Rather than experience withdrawal symptoms that night in jail, most addicts in this circumstance will talk.

Status and reputation

As in many social groups, status among addicts includes the ability to command money, beautiful women, and a big car. Most addicts we met, however, were barely surviving. Their status was determined by their ability to "take care of business," that is, to hustle enough money to maintain their drug habits and to live with a modicum of comfort. Shortchange artists, burglars, and prostitutes could have high or low status depending on how much money they made with their hustle and how little time they spent in jail.

Many people believe addicts are moral degenerates with no social values. We found, to the contrary, that most addicts were very concerned about their reputations among drug users in their community. We learned this the very day we hired Rabbi; he told us he would not do anything for us that would compromise his reputation as being "good people" among his friends at 43d Street. Rabbi, who prided himself on keeping his word, claimed he had never informed on anyone.

During the course of our work at 43d Street, we administered a social status questionnaire in which we asked addicts in this neighborhood to rate one another. We found that among the group given low status ratings were the addicts who would hang out at the wall and literally beg for drugs from dealers and successful hustlers. At the other end of the status scale were the successful dealers and hustlers who would occasionally give drugs to addicts in need—they were considered to be "good people."

Anyone who has worked at an addict rehabilitation center knows the importance of "image" among addicts. Our ex-addict staff enjoyed telling the story about the day Willy Jones came to the admission unit, wearing rags in the dead of winter and with holes in the soles of his shoes, obviously in desperate need of treatment, but strutting about proudly and acting as though he wasn't really sure he wanted it. When staff members told the story they always imitated Willy, standing at the admissions desk with his hands on hips and asking, "You sure this methadone don't cut down your hustling ability?"

Part of the addict's image is the need to be seen with expensive clothes; when their hustle was going well, most did show up on street corners expensively and fashionably dressed. But we came to learn that most had just two sets of clothes—one at the dry cleaner's and the other on their backs.

Violence and social control

Most addicts at 43d Street supported their habits by nonviolent crimes, primarily burglarly, shoplifting, prostitution, and gambling. But the specter of violence followed the addict wherever he went. Because he was engaged in illegal activities, he was not in a position to call the police if he was beaten or "ripped off." Like other criminal subcultures, the addict subculture was ruled by its most violent members.

We have described how heroin dealers must have a reputation for violence, otherwise addicts and other deviants would simply take their drugs and their money. In the communities we studied, most dealers either carried, or had easy access to, guns and knives. By working in pairs or small groups they could beat or injure anyone who caused trouble.

But dealers were not the only source of violence. Deviants of all sorts frequented the addicts' street hangouts, and in these high-crime neighborhoods there was always the risk of confrontation by a drunk, or by members of a delinquent gang who wanted to take away an addict's freshly stolen television set. The addict subculture, outside the law, governed itself by violence.

Some clinicians interpret violence among addicts as an indication of their low frustration tolerance or impulsiveness; but for the addict violence is required behavior for maintaining reputation in the neighborhood, or even in an institution. Rabbi illustrated this in relating a violent encounter in which he had been involved shortly before joining our staff.

"I was sitting in a diner, eating breakfast," he told us, "and in comes this tall young dude who's just come up from down South. He's swaggering and strutting, and he comes and sits down next to me. Now, he knows I've got a reputation, he's heard about me from other people. But he starts to push me—you know, insulting me, making remarks. I told him he'd better cool it, but he kept it up. He was just young and he wanted to prove something. So he kept it up and I told him several times to cool it. I didn't want to hurt him, but finally he just kept it up too long and I had to let him have it. So I just spun around on the counter stool and knocked him down on the floor with my arm, and then I pinned him there, and in my other hand I had this table knife—you know, I had been putting jelly on my toast or something—and I took this knife and I went for his throat, see, but I purposely missed. The knife just went into the floor right beside his neck, so he wasn't hurt, but he was good and scared. Which was all I wanted really. Then I let up on him and he got up and walked out. There wasn't any need for me to hurt him. Just sometimes you have to show people who's boss, that's all there is to it."

Communication

Initially we were intrigued by the continuous talk about dope and street life, but soon this talk became so repetitive that we could not understand how our addict friends could go on and on. Then we realized the function of all the talk. It was important to know who had good dope, who had been ripping people off, and who might be under pressure to inform to the police. So addicts were always asking about one another, partly because of interest and concern for the person, but just as often for practical matters. Who had set up Jaws for his last sale? Was Fat Sam's wife taking over his bag (dealing) now that he was in jail? With no newspapers to keep the addicts informed of subcultural events, they had to keep in constant communication with friends. Information is as valuable to the addict as to the police. When they came to the corner, most addicts at 43d Street would open not with, "Hi," but with, "What's happening, brother?" This was both greeting and invitation for information—perhaps that the corner was under observation by detectives in the grey car up the block, or that a particular dealer would be passing through at two o'clock. Addicts also had special ways of talking with one another when "squares" were present—using code words to let their addict companions know an undercover agent, or a connection, had just entered the bar.

Not all the "jive talk" on Chicago's South Side was so functional. Much of the language and dress was a carry-over from the jazz beat scene of the early 1950s when, as teenagers, these addicts were part of that scene. Had we started our work with white middle-class heroin addicts in a Chicago suburb, we would have encountered the language and appearance of the more recent hippie subculture.

Another unique aspect of the communication system was the universal use of aliases. We were surprised to find that most addicts had known one another for years by their respective street names, but had never been taken to one another's homes or introduced to one another's families. This was a security measure; it is difficult to inform on someone whose real name you don't know. Street names usually had something to do with the individual's personal history or with some unique characteristic. "Foots," for example, walked with a limp and had a slightly deformed foot as a result of a bullet injury he had once incurred while trying to escape from the police. "Jaws" received his name because of his moon-shaped face. Rabbi, who was not Jewish, received his street name from friends when, as a teenager, he wore a black skullcap like a personal trademark. Later as an adult the name continued to fit: "He could always be counted on to do what was right and fair according to the laws of the street ..., always helping dudes when they was down, and even giving stuff away free, if a guy was really desperate and broke."

Our examination of the status, social control, and communication dynamics of the heroin subculture at 43d Street did not, in itself, give us the operational field concepts we sought. Many aspects of this life style were shared by the hip nonaddicts we met at the same corner and could not easily be differentiated from a more general phenomenon—the urban ghetto's hip criminal subculture. This inquiry did serve, however, to make us more sensitive to the realities of the addict's life in the community and less apt to violate the subtle rules of his world when we visited the street.

Geographic Dynamics

Early in our fieldwork we became intrigued with the addict's own framework for viewing his community. He thought in terms of the neighborhood heroin distribution sites called "copping areas." During our own visits to Chicago's high drug-use neighborhoods, we observed that addicts were found not on every street corner but only at very specific locations. We saw the same addicts and dealers at the same sites visit after visit. We wondered if the addict's own concept of the copping area might meet our need for a field research concept.

During the spring of 1969, I personally visited all seventeen of the heroin copping areas in Chicago which had been identified by our field-workers and patient contacts (see fig. 2). All were in black, Mexican, or Puerto Rican neighborhoods, as there were no predominantly white copping areas at that time. The typical copping area in each of the neighborhoods was located in a commercial area with one or more bars, a pool hall, and a restaurant or coffee shop, all of which gave the addicts a reason for hanging out without appearing conspicuous. Copping areas were generally located near major street intersections where public transportation was available. As might be expected, most addicts frequenting a particular copping area shared the ethnic character of the surrounding neighborhood.

Initially, we were surprised at the geographical stability of these copping areas. For example, 43d Street and Langley Avenue had served as a heroin distribution site for the greater part of twenty years. Slowly we came to understand how it must be this way, as the very nature of heroin addiction pharmacologically locks the addict into a local drug distribution system. When he develops withdrawal symptoms, he cannot simply go into the street with his money, hoping to run into a drug dealer; he must know where he can obtain drugs at once. Hence the need for geographically stable drug distribution sites, despite the increased risk this brings from local law enforcement agents.

But a field concept based upon the notion of the heroin copping area would be useful only if we could contact the majority of Chicago's addicts at these sites. We knew addicts who claimed they never purchased heroin on the street but instead used private connections. Thus we were forced to ask the questions, What proportion of active heroin addicts could be contacted at copping areas? How stable is copping community membership?

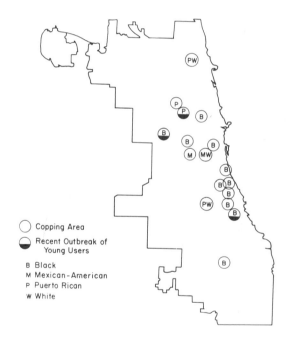

Fig. 2.   Location of heroin addict copping areas in Chicago (Spring 1969)

Questionnaire data from a sample of 156 patients visiting three Chicago methadone clinics on a particular day in 1969 indicated that, during the month prior to entering treatment, 82% frequented street copping areas on a daily basis to buy or sell heroin, another 8% visited copping areas at least once per week, and 2% at least once per month (1% not responding). Only 7%

then, copped or dealt drugs exclusively in private arrangements and would not be identified by a monitoring system that located field staff exclusively at copping areas.

We then asked if we were justified in using the term "copping community"; that is, did most addicts frequent the same copping area on a regular basis? Twenty-three percent of the 156 patients indicated that they had visited only one copping area during the month prior to treatment, 48% had visited two or three copping areas, 16% four or five copping areas, and only 2% had visited six or more copping areas (11% not responding). The majority (60%) also reported that they visited or hung out at one copping area more frequently than others, which on the average they had been frequenting for 4.2 years. These findings held for both Negro and Puerto Rican patient groups. Respondents were then asked to indicate the proportion of addicts frequenting their copping area whom they knew personally. Sixty-one percent of the 154 responding indicated that they "knew" the majority, although only 33% knew the majority by their real names. If this sample were representative of the addict population of Chicago, the data suggested that the majority of active heroin addicts could be reached by a field method locating staff at street copping areas, and that, despite many unstable features of the situation, the regular visitors to these areas might be defined as members of a copping community.

As shown in figure 3, the copping area concept for locating addicts in a community differs from a residency concept as a basis for epidemiological study. Although the majority of the 43d Street copping area members identified at the end of six months lived in the immediate neighborhood (an area with a population of approximately 200,000), the total residency of this group of addicts was distributed over an area with a population of approximately one million. This suggests the advantages of visiting one functional area to initiate and maintain contact with active addicts in contrast to the use of more traditional survey methods. A house-to-house survey, or even a snowball sampling approach, would appear to be much less efficient when we consider that addicts do not usually reveal their real names and addresses even to one another. Our epidemiological approach, then, locates the addict population within a functional and structural framework rather than the more conventional concepts based upon residency or interpersonal links.

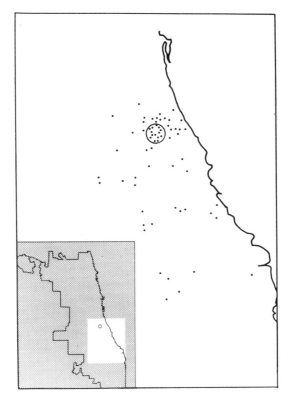

Fig. 3.   Residency of copping community members

Bingham Dai,[13] a University of Chicago sociologist during the 1930s, was the first to note the high frequency with which addicts lived in the immediate area of drug distribution sites. Our findings, 32 years later, support his thesis: 57% of the 63 members of the 43d Street copping community surveyed lived within a one-mile radius. We also found that 54% of the current members of this copping community (22 of the 41 respondents answering this question) first used heroin within one mile of this copping area, a striking finding when we consider that the average duration of heroin use for this group was 15.2 years, suggesting little residential mobility over time.

Role Dynamics

Now that we had brought some definition to the geographical organization of Chicago's heroin subculture, we wondered if it would be possible to define its social organization as well. Stimulated by Preble and Casey's description of the role system in international heroin smuggling, we decided to assign each member of the 43d Street copping community to a functional role vis-à-vis the neighborhood heroin distribution system.

Rabbi began to indicate on his weekly copping area census the functional roles of each addict in the neighborhood. By using the local addict community's own terminology to describe these functions, we were able to assign all members of the 43d Street copping community to one of the dealership roles of big dealer, street dealer, part-time dealer, bag follower, and tout, or to one of the drug consumer roles of hustler or worker.

Big dealers were local wholesalers who supplied street dealers or part-time dealers, although they might sell directly to a few trusted customers. Street dealers sold heroin directly to consumers. Part-time dealers supplemented their income by hustling or working and moved in and out of the dealer role for varying lengths of time. Bag followers simply attached themselves to dealers to support their habits; the three in our study were attractive women who earned their drugs by enhancing a dealer's prestige or by carrying heroin on their persons, since the police are reluctant to search women on the street. Touts carried out liaisons between dealers and consumers, sometimes steering customers to a particular dealer. They would also buy drugs for addicts who had no established connection with dealers. Hustlers engaged in various illegal activities other than drug distribution to support their habits; most commonly they were shoplifters or burglars. Workers maintained at least a part-time legitimate job, although most hustled as well.

This division of labor follows the functional requirements of drug distribution originally described by Preble and Casey.

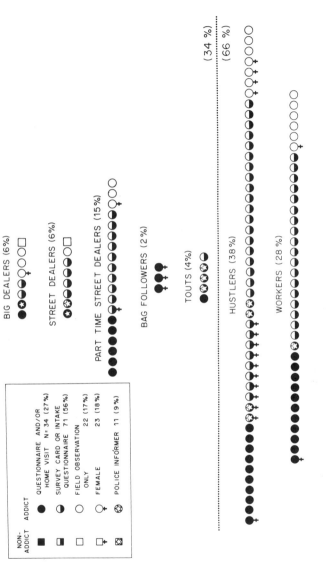

Fig. 4.   Role structure of the 43d Street copping community

However, our classification excluded roles in the distribution hierarchy above the neighborhood level and it also differed slightly from Preble's classification in assigning each person to only one primary role. "Part-time dealer" is the only label that we developed to meet our classificatory need; all the other roles and definitions were based on the current use of these terms by the heroin addicts in our community. Although some members occupied several distribution roles during the period of study, weekly recordings for a four-month period suggested considerable role stability over time.

The distribution of this copping community's membership according to functional roles is portrayed in figure 4. Note that a high proportion, 34%, were primarily engaged in drug distribution. Only two members of the copping community were non-addicted dealers, motivated purely by economic gain. The figure also shows the distribution of women and police informers within the various roles.

Although 127 men and women were active members of this copping community at some time during the twelve months of observation, an average of only 56% visited the area during any given week. New members entered after relapsing into addiction or moving from other copping areas when higher quality heroin became available. Others stopped visiting because they entered jail or treatment. During the last week of August 1969, for example, the copping community had a total of 66 active members: seven big dealers, three street dealers, one bag follower, five touts, 31 hustlers, and 19 workers.

The Copping Area and Copping Community as Field Concepts

Our search for field concepts to operationalize the heroin addict subculture, which started with a very broad examination of the social dynamics of this subculture, gradually narrowed to a set of simple geographical and organizational concepts. For our field concept we adopted the addicts' own "natural" basis for organizing themselves in urban communities, thus permitting us to locate them in a definable social system rather than as isolated social units. It was this search that led (1) to our observation that active heroin addicts were functionally organized into local drug distribution systems, and, as a logical extension of this finding, (2) to the epidemiological principle of organizing field research and intervention activities around these local drug distribution systems.

Our findings suggested that a field team located at neighborhood-level heroin distribution sites could define the membership of these drug-using networks and could obtain sufficient survey and observational data to monitor local incidence and prevalence trends. Additional survey data obtained from a patient sample indicated that the majority could have been reached in this manner prior to entering treatment.

But aside from this empirical support from a sample that may not be representative of Chicago's total heroin addict population, the necessary existence of such stable neighborhood-level heroin distribution structures can be explained on pharmacological grounds alone. Here we point to one of the key features of this disorder—that the host must continuously engage in drug-seeking behavior or, by definition, cease to be addicted. This repetitive drug-seeking behavior, combined with the need for a stable drug source, produces a rather standard drug distribution system, a concrete structure which epidemiologists can map out and perhaps modify through treatment outreach programs.

Reducing the Number of Addicts at Neighborhood Copping Areas

4

Once we had defined the major geographical and organizational dimensions of the addict social system, developing a strategy to count and reduce the number of addicts in target neighborhoods became a rather straightforward matter of trial and error. We chose the 43d Street copping area as the site for launching our first pilot intervention project. Then by subsequent modifications and retesting of our intervention model in other neighborhoods, we gradually approached our end goal of producing the heroin-free community.

A Pilot Intervention Experiment at 43d Street

Rabbi was asked to maintain a census of the regular addict visitors to the 43d Street copping area. This census permitted us to develop a measure of copping area prevalence, which we

Portions of this chapter appeared originally in P. H. Hughes and J. H. Jaffe, "The Heroin Copping Area: A Location for Epidemiological Study and Intervention Activity," *Archives of General Psychiatry* 24, no. 5 (1971): 394–400, and in P. H. Hughes, C. R. Sanders, and E. Schaps, "Medical Intervention in Three Heroin Copping Areas," *Proceedings of the Fourth National Conference on Methadone Treatment* (New York: National Association for the Prevention of Addiction to Narcotics, 1972), pp. 81–83.

defined as the number of active addicts who were regular visitors to this heroin distribution site during any given month of the period of study.[1] For this project, a regular visitor was an addict who was known to buy or sell heroin at this location for at least one month during the period of observation.[2]

In choosing to measure copping area prevalence, we were taking advantage of the natural social organization developed by addicts for heroin distribution. Our measure of prevalence, then, is based not on an addict's residence in a specific geographical area but on his affiliation with a particular heroin distribution site. In other words, some active addicts residing in Rabbi's immediate neighborhood regularly obtained heroin at other copping areas and thus would not be included in our census. Conversely, there were addicts who resided outside Rabbi's immediate neighborhood who obtained their drugs at 43d Street; they would appear in our census of copping area visitors.

After a short pilot period, Rabbi began to maintain systematic records in January 1969. He also requested the regular visitors to complete green survey cards, telling them that by completing these cards they might be included in a special treatment project to be launched in the neighborhood soon.[3] Most copping area members were initially suspicious of the green card, but by the end of six months sixty-three had responded (see fig. 5).

Our strategy for reducing the number of active addicts at the copping area was to offer a selected sample immediate admission to the IDAP treatment system. Generally they would be assigned to methadone outpatient clinics, but a small number might be placed in therapeutic communities or assigned to hospital withdrawal. The decision to assign our subjects to specific treatment modalities and facilities was the responsibility of IDAP clinical staff.

During June 1969, the sixth month of monitoring prevalence, we admitted ten addicts to treatment (see fig. 5). During the next four months, an additional sixteen copping area members were admitted. But monthly prevalence of actively addicted regular visitors did not decline despite our admission of twenty-six active addicts between June and October 1969.

Fortunately, Rabbi had been collecting data on drug availability and law enforcement factors which might affect copping

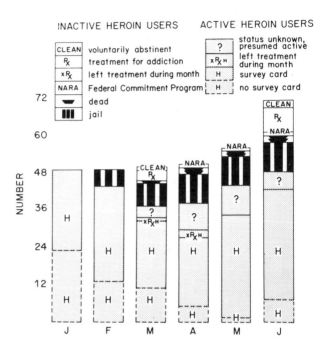

Fig. 5.   Monthly addiction status of copping community members

area prevalence, so we were about to identify some of the reasons for the disappointing results. The primary reason was one of our own making—our intervention activities were conducted over too long a period. Had we wished to demonstrate the intervention effect in a dramatic fashion, we should have admitted all twenty-six addicts during a period of a few weeks. But the project included a home visit and a clinical interview for each addict prior to admission, so we admitted only two or three each week, and their places in the copping area were taken by other addicts who had either relapsed or moved into the area from other neighborhoods. A second factor, equally unanticipated, was the effect of a local teenage gang upon 43d Street copping area prevalence. The "Disciples," whose turf included the 55th Street copping area, began to extort money from the heroin dealers and addicts who met there. The addicts and dealers handled the problem by simply dispersing to nearby copping areas, one of which was 43d Street. A third factor working against us was the arrival in the sixth month (June) of a new dealer with high-quality, low-cost heroin, which again contributed to the influx of addicts from other copping areas.

Actually we considered the overall project in very positive terms; we had developed a methodology for monitoring and reducing copping area prevalence. Furthermore, we had been able to identify factors other than the treatment system that affect copping area prevalence, factors to be considered in designing future intervention projects. We had also conducted the first planned epidemiological intervention experiment in addiction control, using a simple before-and-after experimental design. That is, we could monitor the prevalence of active heroin addicts at a target copping area, then launch an intervention program. If prevalence of active addicts was reduced, we could assume, with certain limitations, that the intervention approach was responsible. If prevalence was not reduced, we were able to identify reasons for this condition and to alter our intervention approach to be more successful in future experiments.

Our original plan called for the initial pilot intervention project to be followed by an all-out effort to involve all heroin addicts at the 43d Street copping area in treatment. Toward this goal the patients we admitted from 43d Street had been assigned to the 79th Street Clinic, where I served as their physician and Rabbi as their rehabilitation counselor. They were to form the patient nucleus of a new clinic which would be established in the immediate vicinity of 43d Street. Rabbi began to make contact with neighborhood organizations and to canvass the area for a suitable clinic location.

Unfortunately this was a time of serious organizational change for IDAP, and we were not able to mobilize sufficient IDAP administrative support to carry this project through to its conclusion. In fact, a decision was made in the fall of 1969, despite our protests, to break up our strongly cohesive group of 43d Street patients and disperse them to a number of different treatment facilities. Our project died.

Lacking IDAP support to continue our work, Gail and I busied ourselves writing up our findings. But our original team was breaking up. I began to look for a more favorable setting to continue the work, Noel accepted a fellowship at the University of Illinois in Urbana, and Rabbi became a full-time counselor at the 79th Street Clinic.

Then in late 1969 we received news of a sizable grant from the National Institute of Mental Health (NIMH). The grant would permit us to accomplish a great deal, even if the situation at IDAP did not improve. I began to recruit additional research staff and Rabbi was screening IDAP counselors and patients to recruit field-workers, when tragedy struck.

Loss of Rabbi

Rabbi was found dead in his apartment. The autopsy showed that he had experienced a pulmonary hemorrhage; there was no evidence that his death had been drug related.

Rabbi's funeral was held just a few blocks away from the copping area and was packed with IDAP staff, patients, and his street friends, some of whom were nodding. Dr. Ed. Senay, who later became IDAP director, delivered a moving eulogy, capturing what Rabbi symbolized, what he represented to the community and to the program.

Dr. John Chappel, director of IDAP Medical Services, expressed what Rabbi's death meant to him in his touching poem "Hey Rabbi!"

In memoriam: Robert Rose, July 1970.

Hey Rabbi!

How much can you hurt? Try counting the ways
And you'll find that your hours soon turn into days.
Death may be the end, but starts things anew
Bringing fresh pain to those caring for you.

Though the wound on the surface may leave a big scar,
The hurt that is hidden heals slowest by far—
Cropping up in strange places with an awesome dread,
Leading others to wish that they, too, were dead.

Survival requires a strong measure of pride,
Producing an image where blues and fears hide.

So you smile and reach out to help others alone,
Covering your needs with a light-hearted song.

It seems so important, living up to that dream,
While a mask of health covers a long, silent scream.
And the tears you could never let openly flow,
Hit family and friends with a terrible blow.

Change never is easy, simple, or nice,
And each spurt of growth comes attached to a price.
You may ache to forever be rid of the blues;
The reality is that you'll always pay dues.

So turn from the coffins, life has to be faced,
And the soul's inner agony can't be erased.
We can cover it up, keep from being aware,
And avoid sharing pain with others who care.

The result will come close to pure living hell,
Little better than death in the street or a cell.
The choice is not easy, it's risky as well,
Do we face sharing pain or retreat to our shell?

Rabbi's death and his funeral profoundly affected all of us. We
had all known our long hours at IDAP were worthwhile, but
somehow his death brought out the full meaning of the program
and our work together at 43d Street. In two short years IDAP had
permitted this man, who had known nothing but prison and drug
dealing during his first forty-five years of life, suddenly to turn
into a dynamic and powerfully constructive force in his community.

During the week that followed we did very little. We were all
torn up inside. We went into the office, but spent most of our
time on busy work. We had come to depend on Rabbi as our eyes
and ears in the community; we owed him so much. Finally, we
realized we would only let him down if we did not continue the
work he believed in.

One of Rabbi's closest friends before his entry into treatment
was another highly placed heroin dealer, Clarence Lawson, better
known among Chicago addicts as "Superman." "Sup," as everyone at IDAP called him, had earned his street name during the
early 1940s when he was only thirteen and a member of the

"Pythons," a gang with headquarters at 43d Street and Vin-cennes. At the time the competing gangs settled disputes and avoided open warfare by letting their strongest member fight the strongest member of the opposing gang. As the Pythons' war minister, Sup never lost a fight. Later, as an adult, Sup continued to live up to his earlier reputation through his extraordinary feats as a drug dealer. It was said that he could fix any case, that he always had advance warning when police were planning to raid him. Whether or not the stories about him were true, his performance as a patient and then as a staff member in IDAP proved him deserving of his title, for eventually he moved up to the position of clinical director of the entire IDAP system. But that was to come later. At the time of Rabbi's death, Sup and he were working together as counselors at the 79th Street Clinic. We asked him to take up where Rabbi had stopped and to help us develop our new team of ex-addict field-workers. Sup loved and admired Rabbi probably more than any of us; there was never any question but that he would accept.

Selecting Neighborhoods and Field-Workers

A major goal of the new series of projects was to determine if we could launch intervention projects in neighborhoods of our choice. To do this, we first chose the copping area, then recruited the field-workers. To make our findings more gener-alizable, we chose neighborhoods with diverse ethnic makeup. One of the two most active copping areas in the black neigh-borhoods of Chicago's West Side was selected. Another was the major street distribution site for Chicago's Mexican addicts. The third site was one of three active copping areas serving Puerto Ricans on Chicago's North Side. The three copping areas were roughly equidistant from IDAP's centralized admission unit, located just west of Chicago's downtown Loop district. At the time of these selections, fall 1970, we knew of no predominantly white copping areas, although whites frequented the Puerto Rican and Mexican sites.

Sup recruited Otis Peek as our field-worker for the black West Side area. This recruitment had presented him with little dif-ficulty, because IDAP had developed its initial programs in

Chicago's black community and we had increasing numbers of highly competent black ex-addict staff members.

Because there were few Mexican patients at the time, however, we had a limited pool of people to choose from. The most likely candidate was a man who was aggressively lobbying for establishment of a methadone clinic near the Mexican copping area selected for study. Unfortunately, his wife, who was also under treatment for addiction, had a history of repeated hospitalizations for psychotic behavior. She gave him a great deal of trouble, and he invariably returned to heroin use when under stress. During these times he would be unreliable, and eventually we had to let him go. Our next candidate was Rio Lopez, who had a stable work history and was making excellent progress as a methadone patient. This was a fortunate choice as he did an excellent job.

For the Puerto Rican–white copping area, we chose Angelo Rivera, a counselor at the North Side methadone clinic. Angelo had good contacts on the streets but he had dropped out of school early and could not write well enough to record his observations. We resolved this by hiring another counselor at the same clinic, Mary Kaye Hubbard, as backup. This worked out very well because this gave us two people thinking about the project, two sources of information, and Mary Kaye did an excellent job of writing up the observations.

Jointly supervising our field-workers were Sup and Clint Sanders. Clint was just completing his sociology graduate studies at Northwestern University, where he had field research training under Howard Becker. He supervised the scientific aspects of data collection, training the field-workers to use similar procedures in recording their observations, and making sure they understood exactly how to code the information they gathered. He also made periodic visits to the areas to make independent observations and to verify field-worker records. Sup's job was to make sure the field-workers, once recruited, remained honest and did not manipulate either the data or the professional members of the research team. He also checked the accuracy of field-worker reports and made sure they were actually spending time on the streets. The concept of dual supervision by an experienced ex-addict and a trained field researcher worked extremely well and may be considered by other researchers in designing studies of drug users or deviant groups in their natural setting.

Intervention Projects

Our field-workers began to maintain their copping area logbooks in the fall of 1970, and by the spring of 1971 we were ready to enter the intervention phase. But IDAP admissions were closed because the program had expanded its treatment capability to the limit of its personnel and economic resources. Finally, in late April, we received word that the new admission unit would open in June: our intervention projects could admit seventy-five patients.

To avoid raising expectations for treatment that we might not be able to meet, we had not distributed survey cards in the copping areas until receiving the go-ahead from the admission unit. When we received the good news, field-workers immediately distributed cards to all monitored addicts in the three areas, and by mid-May approximately two-thirds had returned them completed. The survey cards were important because with the field-workers' logbooks they gave us a data base for defining the populations at the three copping areas. The logs contained observational data only; they did not contain such basic information as age, education, address, or telephone number.

The addict population at the Mexican copping area was relatively small, so we decided to offer the entire group immediate treatment. Since we were not given sufficient treatment slots to admit the large numbers of addicts at the black and Puerto Rican areas, we had the opportunity to select control groups. They would not be offered immediate admission to treatment, but would continue to be observed by the field-worker. If they wished to receive treatment, they would be required to seek it in the usual manner by applying at the admission unit and waiting approximately three months for their names to reach the top of the list.[4]

Response to Outreach

Table 2 shows the response to outreach for the 73 subjects actively addicted in June and known to have received the offer of

Table 2   Addicts Entering Treatment in Response to Outreach

Copping Area	No. (%) Contacted and Available	No. (%) Appearing for Intake during First Month	No. (%) Appearing for Intake within Six Months	No. (%) Admitted during the Six Months
Black	20 (100)	19 (95)	19 (95)	17 (85)
Mexican	29 (100)	18 (62)	23 (79)	20 (69)
Puerto Rican	24 (100)	19 (79)	21 (88)	19 (79)
Total	73 (100)	56 (77)	63 (86)	56 (77)

immediate treatment. Fifty-six (77%) reported to the intake unit in the first month and 63 (86%) within six months. Table 2 also shows, however, that of the 63 reporting for admission only 56 (77%) actually entered treatment. That seven (10%) subjects reported to the admission unit but either did not complete intake procedures or did not report to the assigned treatment unit could be attributed to poor motivation, but field-workers felt that it was in large part due to the frustrations our outreach subjects experienced at the new admission unit.

During the initial month of outreach our field-worker in the Mexican neighborhood, Rio Lopez, expressed disappointment that several of his friends had reversed their decisions to enter treatment. He attributed this to reports from the first outreach subjects to be admitted that there were no Spanish-speaking staff. They met large numbers of black staff and concluded that the program was run by and for blacks, and they felt it would not be sensitive to their needs. Indeed, the percentage (69%) of Mexican outreach subjects actually entering treatment was slightly lower than the other two groups. This was not a problem for the Puerto Rican outreach subjects because the North Side Clinic to which they were assigned was directed by a Puerto Rican ex-addict, and Angelo, our field-worker, was a counselor there. The issue is of considerable importance because it emphasizes the need for a treatment program to appear attractive and responsive to the target population, if it is to involve them in large numbers.

By recording the number of control subjects admitted each month for a period of six months, we were able to estimate the

Table 3   Tendency of Outreach and Control Subjects to Enter Treatment

Copping Area and Outreach or Control	No. Contacted and Available	No. Admitted Each Month in 1971						Total (%) Admitted June–Nov.	No. (% of Total Admitted Remaining in Treatment Nov. 1971
		June	July	Aug.	Sept.	Oct.	Nov.		
Black: O	20	16	...	...	1	...	...	17 (85)	13 (76)
C	19	2	...	2	1	2	1	8 (42)	6 (75)
Mexican: O	29	15	1	3	...	...	1	20 (69)	16 (80)
C	0	...	...	...	...	...	...	...	...
Puerto Rican: O	24	19	...	...	...	...	...	19 (79)	10 (53)
C	27	1	...	2	1	1	...	5 (18)	4 (80)
Total: O	73	50	1	3	1	...	1	56 (77)	39 (70)
C	46	3	...	4	2	3	1	13 (28)	10 (77)

percentage of subjects who would have obtained treatment had they not been selected for outreach (see table 3). Forty-two percent of black controls and 19% of Puerto Rican control subjects were admitted through their own efforts. If control subjects had sought treatment due to an indirect effect of outreach, we might have expected an increase in control group admissions during the fourth and fifth months of the project, due to the three-month waiting list at that time. No such increase was observed.

We also compared the status of outreach and control groups in the sixth month and found a slightly higher percentage of control subjects still in treatment, 77% as compared to 70% of outreach subjects. Comparison of the two groups is difficult due to the small number of controls admitted and because most of these were in treatment for a shorter time at the observation point. Nevertheless, these findings suggested that, in terms of his tendency to remain in treatment, it makes little difference whether an addict seeks out or is sought for methadone treatment.

Impact on Copping Area Prevalence

At each of the three sites, we observed an increase in the number of active addicts, or monthly prevalence, shortly before we began the intensive outreach phase. This was apparently a response to the field team's administration of survey cards. Addicts who might previously have avoided, or at least not been known to the field-workers began to seek them out and thereby became part of the census. Because the weekly census data prior to this period tended to underestimate prevalence, they are not reported in figure 6.

We did not expect to have significant impact at black and Puerto Rican sites because they served large addict populations and we purposely excluded from outreach a sizable number to serve as control subjects. We did, however, attempt to involve all members of the Mexican copping area in treatment. Figure 6 shows that prevalence declined in all three areas immediately after the intensive outreach effort—a significant breakthrough for us because of our earlier failure to demonstrate this in Rabbi's copping area. We note, however, that six months later prevalence in the Mexican and Puerto Rican areas equaled or exceeded the preintervention levels, and in the black area it approached the earlier level.

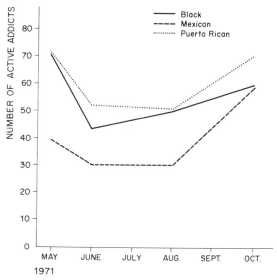

Fig. 6.   Copping area prevalence before and after treatment outreach

We saw several reasons for the failure of these intensive but short-lived efforts to reduce prevalence for longer periods in neighborhoods where addiction was endemic. First, there was a steady return of addicts released from prison or dropping out of treatment. Second, addicts continued to be produced by these neighborhoods. Other reasons were, of course, unique to each neighborhood. For example, in the Mexican area a sizable number of local addicts returned from visits to Mexico and southern border states where they traveled to obtain drugs, to escape inclement weather, or to avoid local enforcement pressures. Thus, intensive short-lived intervention efforts, whether directed by enforcement or treatment agencies, are unlikely to have a sustained effect upon a system which continually receives additional members.

Our intervention projects in three neighborhood copping areas did succeed, however, in demonstrating, first, that our mobile field teams could gain access to active addicts and launch intervention projects in neighborhoods of our choice; second, that our field teams were able to involve three-quarters of street addicts in community treatment programs, and, last, that we were able to achieve short-term reductions in copping area prevalence in all three neighborhoods.

Although we observed that prevalence of active addicts in all three neighborhoods returned to preintervention levels after six months, the reader must recall that our outreach effort was directed at selected subjects chosen several weeks prior to the beginning of outreach. Had we persisted in our outreach activities at the three sites by continuing to offer treatment to additional samples, we would have no doubt produced longer-term reductions in prevalence. In designing future intervention programs, outreach efforts would have to be persistent rather than short-term, if we wished to produce more lasting reductions in prevalence.

A New Challenge

About this time, mid 1971, IDAP's reorganization was completed, and we began to enjoy a period of highly stable relationships with the program. The renewed IDAP support permitted us to follow through on the original program notion for the 43d Street project: an intensive outreach effort to treat all addicts in a target neighborhood. Before we describe the implementation of our final and more comprehensive program model, however, we must point out that 1971 was the year of the Vietnam heroin epidemic, the year when the spread of heroin addiction in our major cities reached crisis proportions. But even before 1971, our attention had shifted to the problem of how to design a treatment system which could intervene in the process of heroin spread. Thus in our next major intervention project, conducted in Altgeld Gardens, a black neighborhood on Chicago's far South Side, we had two program goals: long-term reduction in prevalence of the already addicted, but also reduction in the incidence of new cases in this epidemic community.

Before reviewing the Altgeld Gardens project, it might be useful to examine the dynamics of heroin spread and the problems of measuring the incidence of new cases in communities experiencing heroin epidemics. In this way, we will better understand the rationale we used for designing our intervention approach in Altgeld Gardens.

Reducing Incidence of New Cases

Chicago's Post–World War II
Heroin Epidemic

5   When we initiated our studies in 1968, we were oriented exclusively toward reducing prevalence of chronic addicts. We did not conceive of a treatment program as having impact upon the incidence of new cases.[1] Heroin addiction was generally viewed by American psychiatrists at that time as being one of a number of so-called personality disorders that might be corrected by treatment, but certainly not prevented from occurring. The concept of the addict-prone personality had recently been reinforced by Isadore Chein,[2] who presented convincing statistical data to suggest that addicts have a tendency to be produced in broken homes or in homes with absent fathers and indulgent mothers, particularly in impoverished urban ghettos. Because broken homes, maternal permissiveness, and urban poverty are social factors beyond the power of the psychiatrist to correct on a large scale, it was generally accepted that drug treatment programs would manage those who already had the disorder, leaving the broader task of primary prevention to others. To do otherwise would be a dramatic departure

Portions of this chapter appeared originally in P. H. Hughes, N. W. Barker, G. A. Crawford, and J. H. Jaffe, "The Natural History of a Heroin Epidemic," *American Journal of Public Health* 63, no. 7 (1972): 996–1001.

from the current mental health approach to psychiatric disorders. In other forms of mental illness such as schizophrenia and the psychoneuroses, psychiatrists had not yet demonstrated their ability to prevent the occurrence of new cases of these disorders.[3]

Implicit in the concept of the addict-prone personality is the notion that a given community tends to produce about the same number of new cases in any given period. In other words, most communities have rather stable rates of broken homes and poverty, so that one might expect similarly stable rates of new addict-prone personalities.

We were understandably caught off guard, then, when we found that the year of first heroin-use trends among Chicago heroin addicts followed an epidemic rather than an endemic pattern. In fact, these trends clearly showed that Chicago had experienced a massive heroin epidemic, primarily affecting black youth, immediately after World War II.

We were attracted to the epidemic concept of heroin spread because it had important implications for prevention. Physicians and public health planners have much experience in preventing epidemics of other disorders; perhaps drug addiction treatment programs might have an active role to play in prevention after all. So early in 1969 we decided to study Chicago's post-World War II epidemic, to identify the factors that influenced its course, and to clarify the implications of the epidemic concept for treatment program design.

Documenting the Epidemic

In chapter 2 we described our initial surveys of street heroin users. We found the majority of the first ninety-one adult chronic addicts surveyed had initiated heroin use as teenagers some twenty years before. Intrigued by this finding, we plotted their self-reported year of first heroin use. The resulting trends of first heroin use suggested that the majority of these middle-aged addicts were products of a massive heroin epidemic which began shortly after World War II, peaked about 1949, and declined thereafter. This was a startling finding, so we repeated the survey on a sample of 123 IDAP patients; we found the same pattern. Later we surveyed 715 consecutive black addict admissions to IDAP between May 1969 and September 1970 (see fig. 7). There was no question that there had been an epidemic; it had appeared in three independent samples of chronic heroin addicts.

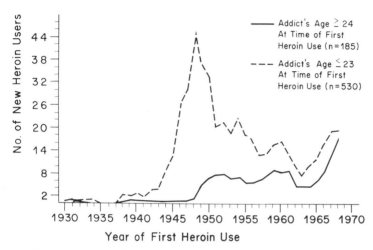

Fig. 7.   Incidence of first heroin use in a black patient sample (1930-68)

We were curious about the events of that period which might explain the etiology of this heroin epidemic and, even more important, the events which might explain the epidemic's sudden decline. To reconstruct these events we interviewed individuals who had worked with addicts at that time: Captain Joseph J. Healey, who had directed the Chicago police narcotics unit during the early 1950s, and Professors Henry McKay, Solomon Kobrin, and Harold Finestone, who had studied young addicts during the period at the Illinois Institute of Juvenile Research.[4] We also examined Chicago newspapers, state legislative hearings, vice and narcotics court records, annual police reports, and Federal Bureau of Narcotics drug seizure data for the epidemic period.

A Historical Account

In his sociological study on opium addiction in Chicago[5] conducted in the early 1930s, Bingham Dai reports that only 17% of Chicago narcotic addicts were black. At that time the majority of narcotic users smoked opium, with only 13% injecting heroin. Reliable addict patients told us that prior to World War II there was limited heroin use in several of Chicago's black neighborhoods. They recalled considerable opium smoking in Chinatown but this involved few blacks.

When World War II disrupted the international heroin and opium trade, addicts were forced to turn to drugstores and physicians for narcotics. During the war, however, domestic marijuana was readily available in the black community and its use was apparently widespread. In 1945 Illinois passed legislation increasing the penalties for marijuana possession, but it did not change the laws controlling heroin; ironically, possession of marijuana became a more serious offense than possession of hard narcotics.

Immediately after World War II, older patients described a polydrug[6] epidemic among teenage blacks in association with a hip youth culture which included jazz musicians and well-known entertainers. Night spots on Chicago's South Side were swinging places for conventioneers and local well-to-do whites; marijuana and heroin became a part of this hip scene and the lyrics of popular songs contained thinly disguised references to drugs. During the late 1940s cocaine use also became widespread.

Heroin was cheap and of high quality, its hazards were not visible or known to new users, and legal penalties were not severe. As Henry McKay observed, heroin use spread from street corner to street corner very much like an infectious disease epidemic. The young people involved, with their colorful and unique "cool cat" life-style, were vividly portrayed by Harold Finestone.[7] At various stages of the epidemic different types of individuals were attracted: for example, the young addicts of the 1940s were hip, street-wise nondelinquents, whereas during the 1950s heroin tended to attract youth with prior histories of delinquency.[8]

The Epidemic's Course

Figure 7 shows that the rapid increase in initial heroin use reversed itself after 1949. Although the decline in first heroin use was not as dramatic as the rise, the downward trend first observed in 1950 continued in subsequent years. While our three survey samples included only about 900 postwar addicts, other accounts suggest that the epidemic produced between five and ten thousand new addicts.[9]

Although we present here data for heroin use only, this was in reality a polydrug-use epidemic. Apparently the epidemic began with marijuana use, followed by heroin, and then cocaine. For example, in a survey of 302 treatment applicants who were involved in the epidemic, first marijuana use preceded first heroin use by approximately three years (mean 1945 vs. 1948, respectively), whereas first use of cocaine occurred approximately two years later (mean 1950). These data point to the rather limited perspective of our inquiry in focusing on the spread of only one drug, heroin, in a large polydrug-use epidemic, and in studying a population limited to only those participants available to us twenty years later as chronic heroin addicts seeking treatment.

One also observed in all three survey samples an upward slope of the first heroin-use curve in the late 1960s (see figs. 1 and 7). At the time of our study we were not sure how to interpret this upswing. A gradually accelerating first heroin-use curve as we approach the present might be expected, even if Chicago's black community produced the same number of new heroin addicts each year, because older addicts are likely to be underrepresented in our samples due to death, imprisonment, other treatment, or "maturing out." In fact, this was not the case and we were indeed detecting the early sign of a massive new epidemic. This epidemic became apparent during the following year, as large numbers of young addicts began to seek treatment. Unfortunately, this was 1969, and we had not yet developed the resources or the field techniques to investigate and intervene in new outbreaks of heroin addiction. All we could do was to launch small-scale pilot intervention experiments as the tragic dimensions of the new epidemic became increasingly apparent. But this is the concern of later chapters and we must return to the concern of this chapter—understanding Chicago's post–World War II epidemic.

The Enforcement Response

As the epidemic moved into full swing, police made an increased number of "narcotic" arrests.[10] The arrest trends in figure 8 show a marked increase in charges against young drug users between

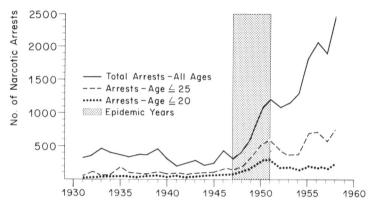

Fig. 8.   Annual narcotic arrests by Chicago police (1931–58)

1948 and 1951, which is consistent with the dramatic growth in the size of the young addict population. The next significant increase in narcotic arrests occurred between 1955 and 1958. This increase does not reflect continued growth in the addict population because arrests in this period fell largely in the over-twenty-five age group. This suggests that the young people originally involved in the epidemic continued to be re-arrested more frequently as they grew older and were not replaced by large numbers of new adolescent addicts. The dramatic increase in arrests in the mid-1950s almost exclusively affected black drug users: between 1953 and 1958 the black/white arrest ratio for narcotic offences averaged nearly seven to one.

It is likely that the increased number of narcotic arrests in 1949 and 1950 reflected a marked increase in the total number of addicts who could be arrested rather than an enforcement response to contain the epidemic. Addict patients reported that during the early phase of the epidemic many police officers did not even recognize the white powder as heroin because the drug had not been widely used prior to that time; patrolmen would take the powder from them, empty it on the ground, and send them home. They also claimed that the few officers who were knowledgeable about drugs were all too frequently corruptible. Furthermore, the City of Chicago Narcotics Bureau was apparently manned by only six to eight full-time officers until 1951, when Captain Joseph Healey was assigned to organize an all-out crackdown on the drug problem. During the next year, the Chicago narcotics force was expanded to sixty officers in the central bureau and sixty more in the local precincts. A standard record-keeping system was initiated for narcotic arrests, and all addict defendants were sent to the central bureau for interrogation. Users received lighter sentences, or had charges dismissed if they would "inform" and help police arrest drug dealers. The result was a heavy and systematic police crackdown on the entire heroin addict population. By 1953 the police had effectively penetrated local drug distribution hierarchies, and it was no longer "cool" to be a heroin addict or dealer in Chicago. The Cook County and city jails were overflowing to the extent that an alcoholic rehabilitation facility was taken over and filled with young addicts.

On the surface it appears that the massive law enforcement response initiated in 1951 was too late to affect the epidemic's course: the peak year of first heroin use in our study population, 1949, had passed two years earlier and first heroin use was already declining in 1950, a full year before the police offensive. The time relationships suggest the police offensive was directed primarily at the aftermath of the epidemic—the thousands of active addicts who were left in its wake. This delayed enforcement response is understandable when one recognizes that one or more years may elapse between the actual peak of heroin spread and the time when the full impact of an epidemic on crime rates is experienced in a given community. For example, one must consider the time that elapses between first heroin use and the development of an expensive drug habit, as well as the time necessary for a young person to become a skilled thief or burglar.[11]

The Legislative Response

In 1935 Illinois approved the Uniform Narcotic Act, which set identical penalties for illegal possession of marijuana and hard narcotics (opium, morphine, heroin). For the first possession offense, the penalty was not more than one year in prison or a $1,000 fine, or both. Because marijuana was the initial drug used in the epidemic, penalties for marijuana violations were greatly increased in 1945; for the first possesssion offense, one to three years imprisonment, or a $1,000 fine, or both. Ironically, the penalties for the possession of hard narcotics were not changed. In 1949, however, the marijuana amendment was repealed and the penalties returned to the 1935 schedule with marijuana and hard narcotics again treated equally.

Note that the heroin epidemic occurred during the same four-year period when repressive legislation was in effect to control increasing marijuana use. Because most addicts involved in the heroin epidemic had previously used marijuana, one might speculate that these sanctions contributed to their shift to a much more dangerous drug, heroin.

Not until 1951 was a bill passed to increase penalties for possession and sale of marijuana and narcotics; in this case it was rushed through the state legislature in thirty-seven days. Penalties were again increased in 1953, with an additional requirement that narcotic addicts must register and carry identification cards. Commonly referred to as the "loitering addict law," it was later ruled unconstitutional by the U.S. Supreme Court.

In 1954 possession of heroin was made a felony, carrying a two- to ten-year sentence; sale of narcotics was punishable by two years to life imprisonment. In 1957, under the Uniform State Narcotic Act, the penalty for the first offense of marijuana or narcotic possession remained two to ten years and a $5,000 fine; first conviction for sale of these drugs carried a mandatory minimum sentence of ten years.

Again we see the response to the epidemic, this time in the form of aggressive legislation, initiated during the period of declining incidence of first heroin use, and therefore directed at the aftermath of the epidemic.

The Judicial Response

Because judicial discretion in sentencing is a form of social control distinct from legislation and law enforcement, we also examined the sentences meted out by judges during the epidemic years.[12] Prior to 1951, many narcotic cases were heard in Rackets Court, branch 27. In 1951 a special Narcotics Court opened in branch 57 of the Municipal District Court.

The sentences in 1948 were relatively light, suggesting that judges were either not aware of the heroin epidemic or had not conceived a punitive response to it (see fig. 9). The trend toward more severe sentences between 1950 and 1956 was consistent with the legislative mandate to increase penalties. Once again we see the pattern of a punitive response reaching its height several years after initial heroin use trends had begun to decline.

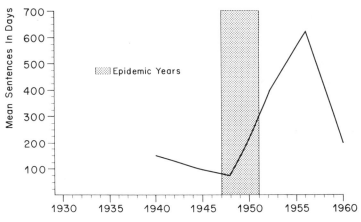

Fig. 9.   Judicial response to narcotic violations (1940-60)

The Therapeutic Response

A number of attempts were made to offer treatment to narcotic addicts.[13] Two hospital wards were opened for narcotic withdrawal, one of them in the Cook County jail; several outpatient counseling clinics were also established. In 1951 the Illinois House of Representatives unanimously passed legislation requiring the Department of Public Health to organize and operate outpatient clinics for addicts in Chicago, but the bill was passed too late in the session for consideration by the Senate. There is some question about how the Senate would have responded, as it had rejected a similar bill earlier in the session.

No government treatment system was established for addiction, and by the mid-1950s local therapeutic responses to the epidemic were largely abandoned because of their uniformly poor results.[14]

Mass Media Response

We reviewed local newspapers of the period in an effort to determine whether public awareness of the "bad side" of drugs might have contributed to the epidemic's decline. We were also interested in relating community concern to the massive enforcement response initiated in 1951.[15]

Beginning in 1948, we found reports of arrests of local black youth, Hollywood entertainers, and jazz musicians on marijuana charges; there was no mention of heroin or cocaine. The year 1950 witnessed a dramatic increase in drug news coverage, which reached a peak in 1951 (see fig. 10). The earlier emphasis on marijuana shifted to concern about "dope" and "addicts." Reports of arrests for possession of drugs were replaced by accounts of daring and violent crimes committed by addicts. One such article described a young man who held up the patrons of a bar; taking the bartender as hostage, he ran into the street and

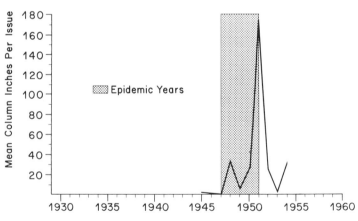

Fig. 10.   Drug abuse news coverage in 120 issues of *Chicago Tribune* (1945–54)

hailed a taxi. While holding a gun on the bartender with one hand, he is described as shooting drugs into his arm with the other.[16]

The news media recorded the changing character of the drug-using subculture. Their descriptions of the "hip" marijuana user of the early stages of the epidemic gave way to portrayals of the "dope fiend" after the introduction of cocaine, a drug which resembles methamphetamine in its effects. When taken in large doses it can lead to violent and paranoid behavior. Assuming that news articles are a measure of public awareness, it would appear that between 1950 and 1952 Chicagoans became increasingly aware of the bad side of drugs and particularly of the audacious crimes committed by addicts. While the influence of community awareness on the decline of the epidemic remains an open question, the news media may have been partially responsible for the massive enforcement response initiated in 1951.

The Cost of Maintaining a Heroin Habit

Reliable patients agree that the cost and quality of heroin available on the street has always been a factor influencing the spread of addiction. To explore this relationship we conducted personal interviews on thirty-five black patients who had been active addicts during the epidemic period. According to them, a heroin habit could be maintained out of pocket money until 1950, when the price almost doubled from the preceding year to $9 a day. This dramatic rise in cost continued to recent years (see fig. 11). Total drug expenditures in the late 1940s may have been somewhat higher than the cost of supporting a heroin habit alone because of the widespread use of cocaine with heroin. But the cost of heroin may have reflected national and international rather than local marketing conditions. We note, for example, that Preble and Casey[17] reported a similar increase in the cost of heroin in New York City beginning in 1951. Prior to that time, young blacks involved in a similar epidemic in that city could support their habits on $2-$4 per day.[18]

We observed similar upswings in the cost of heroin in some Chicago neighborhoods experiencing outbreaks of addiction during the late 1960s and early 1970s, suggesting that such changes

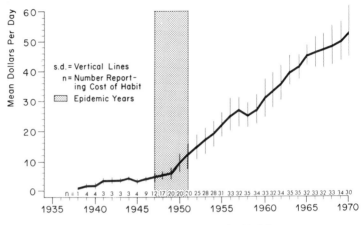

Fig. 11.   Cost of daily heroin habit (1938-70)

in the heroin market may be an intrinsic feature of these epidemics. Thus, during the early contagious phase of an epidemic, when heroin use is primarily experimental, there is no captive clientele requiring a regular drug supply. Once a significant number of the experimenters become actively addicted, however, a stable neighborhood drug distribution system is required. The costs of maintaining such a system are necessarily passed on to the consumer as higher prices, while at the same time dealers find increased opportunities to manipulate drug quality.

The sudden rise in the cost of maintaining a heroin habit suggests a second explanation for the dramatic increase in criminal activities reported by the press in 1950 and 1951. One might expect that the conversion of a hip, fun-loving, drug-abuse subculture into a criminal addict population would be accompanied by an increase in clumsy, and sometimes daring, illegal acts to obtain money.

Purity of Heroin

The influence of drug costs on incidence trends cannot be understood without taking into account drug quality as well. At the time of the post-World War II epidemic, although local police did analyze drug seizures for the presence of opiates, they did not record the purity of opiates in their samples. The Federal Bureau of Narcotics, however, did analyze drug purity and we were able to examine their case reports of heroin seizures in Chicago for the years 1943-70.[19] Since this national level enforcement agency directed its efforts at the higher levels of drug distribution, the seizures analyzed were presumed to be of higher purity than the heroin available to the addict on the street. Nevertheless, there was a decrease in the purity of heroin seized during the period of epidemic decline (see fig. 12). The data also show increased purity of heroin during the late 1960s, which we now know was associated with the heroin epidemic of the late sixties and early seventies.

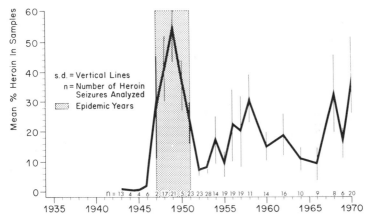

Fig. 12.   Heroin seizures by Federal Narcotics Bureau
(1943-70)

Of the various factors analyzed in the post-World War II epidemic, variations in the purity and cost of heroin appear to have been most directly related to incidence of first heroin use trends. This condition points to drug availability as one probable cause of the rise and decline of the epidemic. Because the purity of heroin available on the street is often related to international marketing conditions, however, it is likely that national and international factors affecting heroin availability were more important in causing the epidemic's decline than the Chicago response.

Value of the Epidemic Concept

The finding that initial heroin use trends can follow an epidemic pattern was a major breakthrough in the efforts of our team to develop operational principles for designing drug-abuse prevention programs. For program planners, the notion of controlling heroin epidemics is a more concrete and action-oriented goal than, for example, trying to correct the presumed social origins of the addict-prone personality—namely, family instability, maternal indulgence, and poverty.

In our analysis of Chicago's post–World War II epidemic we were not able to pinpoint one specific cause of the epidemic or its decline; rather, we identified a variety of factors which may have contributed in varying degrees. We found considerable potential, however, in the analytic framework employed in this study, one which related the time relationships of increasing and decreasing initial heroin use trends to potentially causal events that we could identify and measure. If this analytical framework were used to study other heroin epidemics, we might eventually clarify the specific causal factors that have greatest influence and which might be altered by intervention programs. For example, in this study we found a close relationship between availability of high-quality heroin and increasing speed of initial heroin use. By monitoring first heroin use trends and factors affecting heroin availability in a number of different communities, the precise relationships might be clarified. In time such studies might develop a sufficient body of knowledge to place drug-abuse planners in an operational field in which various programs, policies and approaches could be experimentally manipulated, and their effects upon incidence trends observed.

Planning Treatment Services

The planning of clinical services for epidemic and endemic disorders differs in several important respects. For an endemic disorder, planners expect fairly stable incidence and prevalence rates for a given community over time. For this reason, personnel and program needs also remain fairly stable. For an epidemic disorder, on the other hand, incidence and prevalence may vary greatly from community to community and from year to year in the same community. Programs for the control of such disorders must be established rapidly in areas of need and then phased out as the need diminishes.

In the design of clinical services for many epidemic disorders, it is often not sufficient merely to treat those who have been affected. The treatment program must also address itself to intervening in the process by which the disorder spreads. For example, in venereal disease control it is necessary to treat contagious individuals rapidly to prevent them from spreading it to others.

Epidemic disorders frequently require epidemiological components to be attached to clinical services. In this way there is close coordination between the activities of those who treat the cases already affected and those who correct the factors that are producing new cases.

Clarifying the Natural History
of Heroin Epidemics

Chicago's post-World War II epidemic appeared to have certain characteristics which, if found to be intrinsic features of heroin spread, might suggest specific strategies for their control. In this epidemic there was a tragic time lag between the contagious stage during which heroin use spread and the stage when the epidemic's full impact was felt and reacted to by the host community. Our data suggest the epidemic may have already peaked and been on the decline when the community finally mobilized to control it. In this respect heroin epidemics may differ from contagious disorders with short incubation periods which come to public attention within a matter of days or weeks. During the prolonged incubation-like period of heroin addiction epidemics, there are few signs to alert the community to a growing problem. Even during the early stage of physical dependence, young heroin users are not yet skilled enough in theft and other illegal activities to exert an appreciable effect upon the community's economy.

Once a community accumulates a sizable population of criminal addicts, however, it does feel the burden of maintaining an expensive drug distribution structure. At this stage the community witnesses increasing arrests of new young heroin addicts and begins to identify the nature and extent of the problem. Unfortunately, it then faces the twofold problem of launching prevention programs to halt further spread and of providing rehabilitation services for a large population of active addicts. Thus we see the community responds, not to the early contagious phase of the epidemic, but to the later phase of increasing prevalence of active addicts.

If this formulation of the natural history of heroin epidemics is supported by further research, then it may be more economical and humane for a community to intervene actively during the earliest stages of heroin experimentation by even a few young people, rather than be forced to launch drastic and expensive programs a year or more later to deal with a much larger number of chronic addicts.

But how might a community treatment program go about the practical task of identifying and responding to new outbreaks? To answer this question, it would be necessary to study the dynamics of heroin spread on the neighborhood level. It would be necessary to innovate and test practical strategies by which treatment programs might intervene in heroin spread on the community level where the preventive work must be initiated.

A Model for Researching and Intervening in Heroin Epidemics

6

By early 1970 we were aware that Chicago was experiencing another large-scale heroin epidemic. During our 1969 field visits to Chicago's major copping areas, we had found only two neighborhoods with large numbers of young addicts—the black Lawndale community, and a Puerto Rican neighborhood near Humboldt Park. But one year later we were able to visit five such neighborhoods and we began to see young addicts entering the IDAP treatment system in large numbers.

Fortunately we were just then completing our analysis of Chicago's earlier epidemic of the late 1940s. This enabled us to approach the current problem with some fairly well-developed notions about heroin epidemics. And by this time we had sufficient confidence in our field concepts and techniques for reducing prevalence of active addicts at heroin copping areas that we asked ourselves if we might be able to develop parallel concepts and techniques for reducing the incidence of new cases in epidemic neighborhoods.

We decided to repeat our earlier strategy: first to conduct careful epidemiological studies of the

Portions of this chapter appeared originally in P. H. Hughes and G. A. Crawford, "A Contagious Disease Model for Researching and Intervening in Heroin Epidemics," *Archives of General Psychiatry* 27 (1972): 149–55.

process of heroin spread in the natural setting, then to design and experiment with intervention approaches based on our findings.

Studying Heroin Spread
in the Natural Setting

The epidemiologist can study phenomena surrounding the prevalence of heroin addiction in the natural setting, at any time of day or night, simply by visiting a neighborhood copping area. The incidence of new cases, however, is a more elusive object of study. Because initial heroin use occurs only once for each individual, it is highly unlikely that the epidemiologist can arrange to be present to witness this event. In fact, it is difficult to detect new heroin epidemics before at least some of those involved develop physical dependence, causing them to "surface" either at copping areas or at treatment clinics. For these reasons, studies of the process of heroin spread might have to be conducted retrospectively, obtaining key data through interviews of recently addicted individuals.

To give our inquiry the broadest possible perspective, we selected young addicts in the IDAP treatment system from a variety of Chicago neighborhoods and ethnic groups. In addition to interviewing the new addict himself, we asked him to help us contact those who were his friends at the time he first used heroin. More specifically, we wished to interview one friend who had only experimented with heroin and had not gone on to addiction, and another friend who was exposed to heroin use but had never tried it. By interviewing more than one participant in the process, we hoped to develop a more complete picture of how heroin spreads in a particular neighborhood. By interviewing addicts, heroin experimenters, and non-heroin users from the same peer group, we hoped to develop some notions about why some individuals who are exposed try it, while others resist, and why some who experiment go on to become addicts, while others do not.

In addition to interviewing members of peer groups in different stages of the addict career, we wished to interview young people from neighborhoods with relatively large outbreaks of addiction, with relatively small outbreaks, and with only one or two cases of addiction. We hoped, thereby, to develop notions about why an epidemic in one neighborhood may eventually produce a hundred or more young addicts, while in a nearby neighborhood heroin spread may stop after producing only one or two new cases.

For purposes of discussing the relative size of heroin epidemics in different neighborhoods, we rather arbitrarily developed the following terminology: we used the term "macroepidemic" to describe a neighborhood outbreak of fifty or more new addicts in the span of five years, "microepidemic" to describe outbreaks of less than fifty but more than two addicts in five years, and "isolated case" for outbreaks in which only one or two individuals become addicted.

The final design of the study then, included fifteen heroin addicts, fifteen experimenters, and fifteen exposed nonusers.[1] The semistructured personal interviews of addicts, experimenters, and non-users were conducted at any convenient location; they lasted approximately two hours and were tape-recorded.[2] They assessed a variety of social and psychological variables, such as family background, neighborhood conditions, peer group dynamics, prior drug use, and police contacts. Subjects then assisted us in constructing a heroin spread diagram similar to that developed by Richard de Alarcon in his study of heroin spread in a British community.[3]

Distribution of New Outbreaks in Chicago Neighborhoods

On the basis of epidemiological field observations, patient interviews, and IDAP admission data, we identified eleven macroepidemics in Chicago between 1967 and 1971 (see fig. 13); nine were in black neighborhoods and two in mixed Puerto Rican–white neighborhoods. The largest outbreaks occurred in economically disadvantaged communities. In addition, we identified twenty-eight microepidemics: fourteen in black neighborhoods, twelve in white neighborhoods and suburban areas, and two in Puerto Rican–white neighborhoods. Outbreaks in suburban areas are not shown in figure 13. Although we probably did not

identify all such heroin outbreaks, it appeared that many Chicago
neighborhoods of similar population size produced either isolated
cases of addiction or none at all.

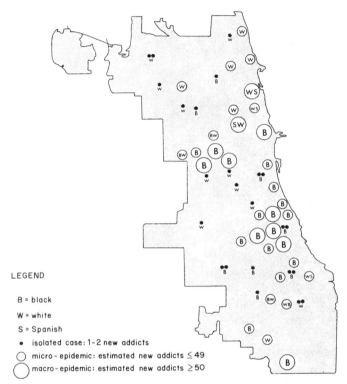

Fig. 13.   Location of macroepidemics, microepidemics, and
                              isolated cases in Chicago (1967–71)

To determine the relative proportions of new addicts involved
in the three sizes of outbreak, we administered an epidemiological questionnaire to the 365 addicts applying for treatment
between January and October 1971 who reported first heroin use
as 1967 or later. On the basis of their residence in one of
Chicago's 76 community areas[4] at the time of first heroin use, we
determined the proportions of subjects whose first use occurred
in macroepidemic, microepidemic, and isolated case neighbor-

hoods. We found that 204 (56%) appeared to be the products of macroepidemics, 137 (37%) the products of microepidemics, and 24 (7%) to be isolated cases. These data suggested that the majority of addicts were produced by macroepidemics which occurred in a relatively small number of neighborhoods.

Isolated Cases, Microepidemics, and Macroepidemics

We modified the approach developed by de Alarcon to portray diagramatically the spread of heroin use in localized epidemics. Because he studied an isolated outbreak in one small community, he was able to obtain data on the majority of those involved and to present a comprehensive picture of the dynamics of heroin spread in one suburban area. Although we attempted to obtain reports from two or more individuals involved in each outbreak, our data were necessarily less complete than de Alarcon's.

Figures 14, 15, 16 portray examples of the three patterns of heroin spread. The history of these outbreaks are not described here in detail but are presented briefly to illustrate the kinds of information that can be obtained by this approach.

An Isolated Case

Figure 14 shows an isolated case of heroin addiction in a white neighborhood. The arrow indicates the direction of spread, while the letters refer to the characteristics of the spreader at the time he initiated the new user to heroin. The symbols indicate the individual's eventual addiction status—heroin addict, experimenter, or non-user. For example, the isolated case shown in the figure was initiated to heroin use in 1966 by a relative (R), who was experimenting (E) with heroin and was also a drug dealer (D). The spreader, in this case the interviewee's sister, had been introduced to heroin previously by her boyfriend, a drug dealer who lived in a nearby neighborhood. Of the isolated cases interviewed, we found that many were initiated to heroin use by a sibling or spouse. We also noted that this interviewee had no close friends at the time she first tried heroin. This was found to be a common characteristic among isolated cases and may account for their failure to spread heroin use to others.

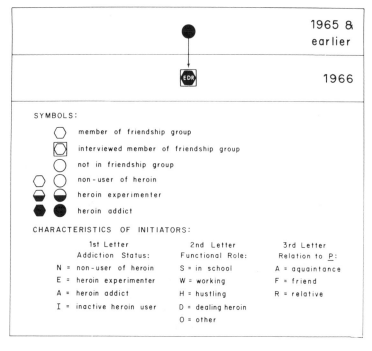

Fig. 14.   An isolated case

A Microepidemic

The microepidemic shown in figure 15 occurred over a five-year period, in a middle-class white suburb. It began in 1967, while most members of the friendship group were still in high school. Their drug use had started several years earlier with alcohol and marijuana, followed by barbiturates, amphetamines, and psychedelics. Prior to the introduction of heroin, then, group members were already heavy multiple drug users. It is interesting to note that even in this relatively small outbreak, heroin was introduced to the group from multiple sources. In addition, members of the friendship group were introduced to heroin in 1970 in three different states, Illinois, Utah and California, a situation which points to the geographic mobility of today's white middle-class youth. When the members of this group eventually returned home, they joined one another in the common pursuit of heroin.

The young people involved in this microepidemic were introduced to heroin, not by a sinister drug dealer, but by their close friends who wanted to share a new high. Thus, in fourteen of the seventeen initiation experiences recorded in the figure, friends supplied the drug. Furthermore, in nine cases the initiators themselves were in the preaddiction or experimental stage, and in the remaining eight cases, the initiators had only recently become addicted. Initially, we postulated that drug-using friendship groups provide the structure through which heroin spreads. Although we did see this pattern in some neighborhoods, it was more common to find multiple and independent sources of heroin introduction from nongroup members.

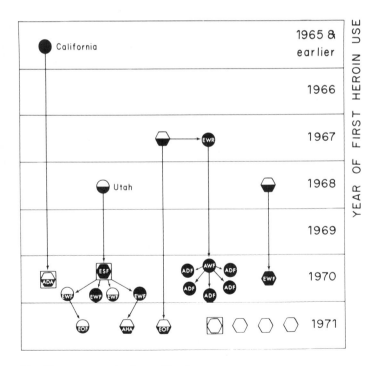

Fig. 15.   A microepidemic

During the early stages of their heroin experimentation, members of this microepidemic, as in other middle-class suburban areas, frequently carried out drug transactions in their parent's homes and at community meeting places of young multiple drug users. For this suburban area, the major hangout was a nearby forest preserve. During the preaddiction phase of this microepidemic, then, the sociogeography of heroin use and distribution resembled that of multiple drug using friendship groups. As group members developed physical dependence upon heroin, however, their drug use and distribution activities increasingly took on the characteristic features of illicit heroin maintenance systems observed in the inner city (see chap. 3). The unique character of these systems is largely determined by the pharmacology of the disorder, namely, the addict's need for heroin every four to eight hours to prevent the discomfort of withdrawal symptoms. Once they are addicted, members of microepidemics become pharmacologically locked into frequent association with other heroin users in the area to maintain a stable drug distribution system.

At this stage of the epidemic, the need for repetitive association with other addicts in the community increases the group's vulnerability to local police surveillance. In this neighborhood, for example, those who traveled daily to the center city to cop heroin for the group soon experienced the hazards of selling drugs at their residences—search warrants can be easily obtained and, when drugs are found, convictions are usually assured. Thus they were forced to move out of their parents' homes and to sell drugs from their own apartments or at local hangouts. During the early stages of a suburban microepidemic, then, young people may experience a "honeymoon" period when the use of heroin is defined as fun and is enthusiastically promoted among friends. With the passage of time, however, these groups begin to experience the continuous fear of arrest, the economic difficulties, and the disruption of family life that are currently associated with illicit heroin addiction in the United States.

Figure 15 suggests that this microepidemic was passing into a less contagious phase after a period of rapid spread in 1970. At the time of our interviews, it appeared that this outbreak would soon be contained. The group was experiencing considerable police pressure; three members had left the community, two had died, and five had entered treatment.

A Macroepidemic

The macroepidemic shown in figure 16 occurred in Altgeld Gardens, an underprivileged black neighborhood with a population of approximately 10,000. The vertical lines in the figure separate five independent friendship groups identified in this macroepidemic neighborhood, suggesting that macroepidemics might be viewed as aggregates of microepidemics.

The large friendship group shown on the left in the figure began to experiment with alcohol while in their early teens. This was followed by the use of marijuana and later barbiturates, amphetamines, and codeine cough syrup. Again we see an adolescent friendship group heavily involved in multiple drug use prior to the introduction of heroin in 1965. The first member of the group to try heroin began experimenting while living in another Chicago neighborhood which had an active heroin copping area. His best friend had tried heroin the day before and described it as a "boss high." On this occasion the two decided to get high together. As this subject explained, "When I found out my friend did it, I made up my mind I was going to try it too." They sought out two older addicts in the neighborhood who copped for them at a cost of $12 each. These addicted acquaintances then accompanied them to a hotel bathroom, "cooked up" the drug, and injected it into the subject and his friend. Other members of this group were subsequently initiated to heroin use by friends who were already experimenting with the drug. Not surprisingly, we again see multiple points at which heroin is introduced, for there are many sources of drugs in this neighborhood.

As members of these independent friendship groups became addicted, they were forced to associate with each other and with other new addicts in the neighborhood for the common pursuit of heroin. The original friendship groups became less cohesive as these young addicts developed new associations based upon the need to maintain their heroin habits. Finally, as the addict

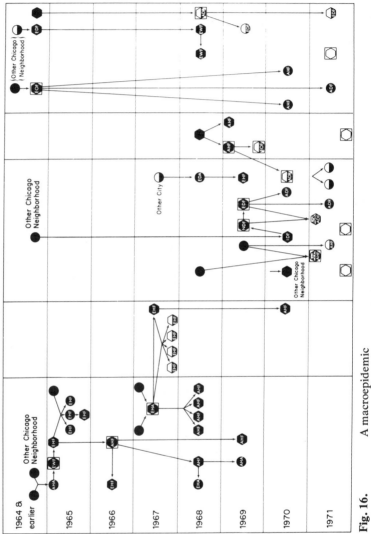

Fig. 16. A macroepidemic

population of the neighborhood continued to grow, an increasingly stable heroin distribution structure developed; addiction now appears to be endemic to this community.

In our study of the macroepidemic shown in figure 16 we had identified 48 addicts and 16 heroin experimenters through our interviewing technique. Additional evidence for a macroepidemic in this neighborhood came from IDAP admission data, which showed 37 new addicts from this neighborhood had applied for treatment. For this analysis, a new addict was defined as a treatment applicant reporting first heroin use between 1967 and 1971.

On the basis of our interviews, field observations, and program admission data from other Chicago neighborhoods, we felt confident that all eleven macroepidemic neighborhoods shown in figure 13 were indeed experiencing sizable outbreaks of heroin addiction. For example, by January 1972 we had obtained admission data on 50 or more new addicts in three of the eleven macroepidemic areas; in four areas we had applications from 40 or more new addicts, and in three areas from 30 or more new addicts. Only one of the macroepidemic neighborhoods had fewer than 30 new addict applicants, and in this case 25 had applied for treatment.

Circumstances Surrounding
First Heroin Use

Our research procedures for studying the process of heroin spread also permitted us to examine the specific setting and social circumstances of first heroin use. At a time when the heroin habits of Chicago addicts ranged from $30 to $80 per day, we were surprised to find that the majority of our interview sample of addicts and experimenters had obtained their first "taste" of heroin free. One plausible explanation is that because the initiators themselves tended to be new experimenters, or recently addicted, they did not have expensive habits to support. Consequently, they did not hesitate to share a new high with their friends.

Although we occasionally heard of a large group of young people "turning on" for the first time at a gang meeting or at a party, initiation to heroin usually occurred in a small group setting, involving only the new user and one or two addicts or experimenters. Most frequently, the initiate was introduced to heroin when he met a friend who was on his way to cop or was preparing to "fix"; he rarely sought out the drug the first time. Thus, initiation depended more on fortuitous circumstances than on a willful act by the new user, or at least this was the case at the time of our study.

Testing an Intervention Model

Contagious disease control strategies have frequently been based upon careful analysis of the epidemiology of disease spread. Similarly, our research has clarified several distinctive features of the process of heroin spread relevant to designing an intervention strategy. First, the disorder tended to be most "contagious" during the early stages; it was spread by new users and by the newly addicted. This suggested that if new outbreaks were identified early and all new cases were then rapidly treated, they would no longer be contagious and further spread might be prevented. Second, the disorder was spread through person-to-person contact, and the individuals involved tended to be close friends or relatives. Third, the maintenance of a heroin habit brings new addicts into frequent association with others in the neighborhood, even though they may not have known one another prior to their addiction. These latter two features suggested that the initial case identified in a new heroin outbreak might be used to lead the epidemiologist to others involved, a standard case-finding principle for some communicable disorders. The feasibility of this case-finding approach was also suggested by our previous survey of 365 young addicts admitted to IDAP, which showed that the majority would be willing to assist the program in involving their friends in treatment. The use of known heroin addicts as case-finding agents had also been demonstrated in two independent studies of narcotic addicts in England, suggesting that this technique may have widespread applicability.[5]

To test the feasibility of such an early identification and intervention model, Gail Crawford stationed herself at the IDAP Intake Unit to screen new admissions. Our aim was to identify and intervene in a microepidemic that had not yet been contained. During the first week of this project, she identified several cooperative subjects from active microepidemics. We selected one of the microepidemics for intervention because of the enthusiasm of the initial contact and because of the proximity of the outbreak to a treatment facility where I personally served as the program physician. The second week of the project was devoted to identifying the individuals involved in the outbreak and to planning the intervention strategy. Then, from the third through the sixth week, we launched an intensive outreach effort. Our initial case contact was hired as the field-worker to assist us in reconstructing the history of the microepidemic, in contacting other individuals involved, and in arranging visits to the local drug distribution sites.

This microepidemic occurred in South Shore, a previously white middle-class neighborhood which was experiencing in-migration of middle- and lower-class blacks. The period of most rapid heroin spread was 1968-70. Members of this group of young white addicts began experimenting with alcohol, codeine cough syrup, and marijuana in 1966, while most were still in high school. This was followed by a period of heavy use of barbiturates and then amphetamines in 1967 and 1968. In 1967 some members of the group also began to experiment with psychedelics, and by the end of 1968 most of these young people were frequent users of lysergic acid diethylamide (LSD). Initially, group members used heroin to "bring them down" from LSD trips. They continued to merely experiment with heroin until early 1971, when several members established connections for copping high-quality Mexican heroin. Thereafter, their drug use was confined mostly to heroin, and by the end of the summer of 1971 most had acquired heroin habits.

At the time of the outreach project, January 1972, our target group consisted of fourteen active addicts and seven regular heroin experimenters. During the previous year, the epidemic had produced an additional twenty-four addicts; however, ten of these had already entered treatment, six had left the neighborhood, and eight others had either withdrawn themselves from heroin or seldom used it. These twenty-four and an additional group of nine occasional experimenters judged to be peripheral to this group were excluded from our outreach efforts.

During the third through the sixth weeks of the project, we

were able to involve in treatment eleven of the fourteen active addicts selected for outreach. Of the three who did not respond, two were shortly arrested, through no connection with our project, and one left the neighborhood. Of the seven regular experimenters selected, five were admitted to treatment, and the remaining two were reported to have discontinued their heroin use. So far as we could determine, active heroin use and distribution was eliminated from this neighborhood.

Our initial efforts had been concentrated on involving in treatment those persons who copped for others. After entering treatment these subjects were no longer willing to cop for their friends, and heroin was no longer available in the neighborhood. Experimenters virtually ceased using the drug. The outreach subjects had been converted from potential spreaders of the disorder to a therapeutically oriented force which actively discouraged heroin use in the neighborhood.

During the first two weeks of this project, we had depended upon our initial contact for a description of the nature and size of this microepidemic. During the four weeks of intensive outreach, however, we made personal visits to the major drug distribution sites in the neighborhood and interviewed all sixteen subjects entering treatment. Their independent and convergent accounts of the microepidemic and of the individuals involved gave us confidence in the accuracy of our data.

Follow-up

Immediately following our outreach project in the winter of 1972, the heroin scene among young whites in South Shore had pretty much disappeared. Once the "main element" of the heroin scene was removed, most of the occasional experimenters remaining in the neighborhood abandoned heroin use. The majority of young people who had entered treatment eventually moved out of the neighborhood, partly due to new interests, and partly due to a more general out-migration of whites and in-migration of blacks.

In the fall of 1972, however, heroin use began to spread again among whites in South Shore. Two brothers were the key instigators in the resurgence of the epidemic. They had been only peripheral members of the original heroin scene, but they subsequently learned where to cop heroin from a third, older brother who was already a user. They gradually drew in more and more people, so that at the time of the follow-up in November 1973,[6] the heroin scene consisted of approximately fifteen addicts who visited the pool hall daily and another twenty regular experimenters. This was a new generation of heroin users who were primarily in their late teens and early twenties.

The major conclusion to be drawn from the follow-up is that a short-term intensive treatment-outreach effort was able to break up one generation of new addicts, experimenters, and their copping network. But without persistent outreach efforts heroin began to spread again, and within twenty months of effective intervention, a new generation of addicts and experimenters had been produced.

The Peer-Contagion Dynamic
of Heroin Spread

Through our interviews with young people involved in localized heroin epidemics we found that the multiple drug using friendship group served as fertile soil for the growth of heroin addiction. While all members of these friendship groups did not become addicted, the majority usually tried heroin after it was introduced. It is important to note that these young people were not simply occasional marijuana smokers prior to their use of heroin. Rather, they tended to be heavy multiple drug users who spent much of their leisure getting high. Over time, group members developed multiple contacts with illegal drug markets, so that periodically heroin became accessible.

We found de Alarcon's method for mapping heroin spread useful in examining local incidence of first heroin use trends over time and in clarifying the processes of social contagion—that is, the specific interpersonal routes of heroin transmission, the characteristics of heroin spreaders, and the circumstances surrounding initiation to heroin use. Because de Alarcon's study investigated spread in a community previously free of heroin, however, it was not directly applicable to a large American urban area where heroin addiction, particularly in the black and Spanish-speaking ghettos, was long-standing. In this study, we were not able to identify discrete epidemics with only one or two sources of contagion. Rather, there were multiple sources of drug availability in localized heroin outbreaks in Chicago during the period of study.

We can do little more than speculate as to why some neighborhoods provide the settings for microepidemics and others for macroepidemics. It is our impression that microepidemics can occur in any type of community as long as the essential ingredient, the multiple drug using friendship group, is present. In this respect, they do not differ from macroepidemic neighborhoods. We noted, however, that macroepidemics generally occurred in neighborhoods that had recently undergone rapid population change, leading to a breakdown in community stability and established mechanisms of social control. In other words, not only had heroin addiction become rampant in these neighborhoods, but so had other forms of deviance as well.

The first two macroepidemics to come to our attention occurred not in the old "dope" neighborhoods of Chicago but in previously stable communities which had recently experienced a massive influx of welfare and "multiproblem" families. This led us to hypothesize that macroepidemics were not occurring in the old dope neighborhoods because of long-established police penetration. Although we later saw large outbreaks of heroin addiction in some of these neighborhoods, this did not necessarily disprove our hypothesis. During the late 1960s several of these communities had been extremely hostile to local police and a number of officers had been killed. This hostility made it both difficult and dangerous for narcotics agents to identify and penetrate new groups of heroin users.

While the foregoing discussion of police-community dynamics is largely impressionistic, we do have some data which bear on this issue. For example, we found young addicts from macroepidemic areas tended to be arrested for property crimes outside their own neighborhoods, while their counterparts from microepidemic areas tended to be arrested for drug offenses within their communities of residence. This finding suggests that aggressive narcotics law enforcement was possible in the more stable neighborhoods and may have been an important factor in limiting the size of these outbreaks.

In this chapter the terms "contagious," "macroepidemic," and "microepidemic" are used frequently. In applying such communicable disease terms to the epidemiology of heroin addiction, however, we must be alert to their limitations. Heroin, to start with, is a chemical substance and not a bacteria or virus. Furthermore, initial use of heroin is almost always a deliberate act and this is rarely the case in the transmission of infectious diseases. Nor does our use of communicable disease principles for early identification and intervention suggest the applicability of quarantine systems for halting heroin spread. Our ability to enlist the cooperation of new young heroin addicts to involve others in treatment was based on their desire to help rather than punish their friends. In the South Shore neighborhood of Chicago, where these principles were tested with considerable success, admission to treatment was strictly voluntary and coercive measures to involve the target population were not necessary.

Prevention and Early Intervention

Our studies of heroin epidemics on two community levels—the large metropolitan area discussed in chapter 5, and the urban neighborhood described in this chapter—have pointed to both planned and unplanned events that might halt heroin spread. For example, one factor that may limit the size of outbreaks in microepidemic areas is the size of the already existing multiple drug using population, a hypothesis suggested by our finding that heroin seems to spread among experienced multiple drug users.

Furthermore, the individuals involved in a particular microepidemic cannot exist as independent social units. Their need for a continuous heroin supply requires that they interact as members of a common social system. Therefore, the removal of one or more key members of the distribution structure in a microepidemic, whether by enforcement or treatment agencies, frequently disrupts the entire social system until the members establish new sources of drug supply. In macroepidemic neighborhoods, on the other hand, the removal of one or more key distributors should have little disruptive effect on the system as a whole because heroin is available from multiple sources. Macroepidemics produce sizable populations of heroin addicts who tend to remain in their neighborhoods of origin despite extensive enforcement pressure. Usually they establish local street copping areas, and thereafter addiction becomes endemic to the neighborhood.

In the following chapter we shall describe our attempt to intervene in such a community—a neighborhood experiencing a macroepidemic. This project, the "Altgeld experiment," was conducted simultaneously with the research described in this chapter, but it is a more complex model because it addresses itself to the long-term reduction of both incidence and prevalence of heroin addiction, and it incorporates the added dimension of community involvement.

Containing a Heroin Epidemic
in Altgeld Gardens

7

During the summer of 1970, our epidemiological field team had identified sizable outbreaks of heroin addiction in five Chicago neighborhoods. Of these five, we chose Altgeld Gardens, a predominantly black public-housing project, to test a community treatment program model for halting heroin spread. One reason we chose Altgeld was that IDAP had at that time admitted only a few patients from this area, so the epidemic was relatively free of treatment program influence. In addition, this community of approximately 10,000 had clear geographic boundaries. It was separated from other Chicago neighborhoods by factories and open fields. We felt this would simplify case finding and permit us to better monitor the events affecting the epidemic's course. We planned a four-phase intervention model:

Phase 1: epidemiological field investigations. Upon contact with the first case in a new outbreak, an intensive case-finding effort is launched to assess the size and other parameters of the epidemic.

Phase 2: pilot outreach and treatment. An

Portions of this chapter appeared originally in P. H. Hughes, E. C. Senay, and R. Parker, "The Medical Management of a Heroin Epidemic," *Archives of General Psychiatry* 27, no. 5 (1972): 585–91.

epidemiological field team attempts to admit to treatment a sample of those involved to determine the most appropriate modalities and locations for treatment services. Efforts are made to develop community support and participation.

Phase 3: intensive outreach and treatment. Attractive and convenient treatment services are provided to meet the needs of all addicts in the community, and outreach efforts are made to involve those who do not actively seek treatment.[1]

Phase 4: follow-up and prevention. Persistent outreach efforts are directed at those who resist treatment, and there is a rapid outreach response when new cases develop or when treated cases relapse.[2] The local community is involved in prevention programs to the extent possible.

In this chapter we shall evaluate the effectiveness of this model over a four and one-half year period (July 1970–December 1974). At the time of this writing, the project is still active.

Implementing the Project

Phase 1: Epidemiological Field Investigation

Based upon field staff reports of a sizable heroin outbreak, I visited the major heroin distribution site in Altgeld Gardens in July 1970. Dick Parker, an anthropologist who subsequently evaluated this project, accompanied me. Our guide was a recently admitted methadone patient, Spellmon Young, who was highly respected and trusted by the addicts in the neighborhood. On that initial visit we met enough young addicts to justify a project and shortly hired Spellmon as the epidemiological field-worker.

Spellmon's first function was to maintain a census of all addicts in the community and to make weekly recordings of any changes in their addiction status. By October 1970 he had developed an active census of forty heroin addicts, the majority of whom were teenagers or in their early twenties. Spellmon's association with the treatment program permitted him to invite Clarence Lawson, Dick Parker, and other members of our research team to addict hangouts in the area to check the accuracy of his reports and to make additional observations.

Phase 2: Pilot Outreach and Treatment

In January 1971 Spellmon approached several influential members of the young addict group and offered them immediate admission into the treatment unit nearest their residence. This demonstrated the legitimacy of his helping role and also gave us experience with the practical problems of outreach and the unique treatment needs of the target population. We were disappointed to find, however, that several of the youngsters who had expressed interest in treatment never reported for intake and later complained of transportation difficulties. Upon examination, this complaint proved legitimate. Public transportation to the nearest clinic involved a round-trip fare of $2.00 and traveling time of one and a half hours.

Phase 3: Intensive Outreach and Treatment

The discouraging results of our pilot phase reinforced our impression from earlier projects that we would have little impact on the epidemic unless treatment services were located in the community and were attractive to the target population. During the spring of 1971, we entered into discussions with representatives of the Altgeld-Murray Community Council to establish a multimodality treatment and rehabilitation facility in the neighborhood.[3] When agreements were formalized in July 1971, we admitted twelve high-status young addicts into a residential therapeutic community at some distance from the neighborhood. We hoped to recruit future staff members for the community facility from this group.

In November 1971, the "Day One" clinic opened its doors in Altgeld Gardens. Community resistance was limited to a few residents immediately adjacent to the facility, and this was overcome through an active public relations effort by Spellmon and the solid support of the Community Council. Spellmon shifted from epidemiological field-worker to program director. When the clinic opened we recruited five counselors and an additional epidemiological field-worker from neighborhood residents previously admitted to the therapeutic community. Nursing staff was recruited from community residents, and we were able to involve, as the clinic physician, a young black woman who had been working with the Community Council to improve local medical services. New patients were admitted at the rate of approximately four per week, until March 1972, when intake dropped to one or two per week.

Phase 4: Follow-up and Prevention

In March 1972 we entered into a series of discussions with the Health Committee of the Community Council to review systematically with clinical and field staff our efforts to involve sixteen active addicts who continued to resist our outreach efforts. Some of these resistances were easily overcome. We discovered that six of the older addicts were reluctant to come into the clinic because of the young age of staff members. We solved this problem by asking Spellmon, the only middle-aged staff member, to serve as the counselor for these individuals.

Suggestions were occasionally made at meetings that police pressure or eviction from public housing might be used to rid the community of the most resistant addicts, but these actions proved unnecessary. By late April, only eight active addicts remained, three of whom were hard-core drug dealers. Without a sizable heroin market to support their drug habits, four of the active addicts entered the program and two moved from the community. In July the remaining two addicts not in treatment shifted to methylphenidate hydrochloride (Ritalin) abuse and became irregular users of heroin.[4] During August 1972 representatives of the community organization and program staff began to shift their attention to planning rehabilitation services for multiple drug users and drug education programs for the local schools.

Once we had delivered the addicts of this community to the clinic, the question shifted to one of rehabilitation: could the treatment system maintain a heroin-free community? Spellmon Young, the clinic director, was a charismatic and innovative individual who launched an active program to keep the patients involved. He approached local industries to employ his patients and obtained funds to purchase a laundry business where they could obtain work experience. He approached employment and vocational training agencies, and by October 1972 he had achieved a degree of success: sixteen patients were working, ten of them as counselors in the IDAP system. But the majority were in approximately the same position they were in when they first turned to heroin—they were black, poorly educated, and isolated from job opportunities.

In November 1972 the Altgeld-Murray Community Council and IDAP convened a "job fair." This was a meeting of local, state, and federal representatives of vocational rehabilitation and employment agencies in a desperate effort to come to grips with the unemployment problem. Despite much discussion and exchange of ideas and advice, the result after several months was continued discouragement—and no new jobs. Spellmon was showing the strain and, with considerable relief, he accepted an IDAP promotion in August 1973, handing over responsibility for the Altgeld program to his highly competent assistant director, John Turner. Although John pursued the previous orientation, he met with no greater success and morale of staff and patients continued to decline. The outreach public health orientation— keeping people involved in treatment and reaching out to reclaim them if they dropped out—was gradually lost. The clinic came under increasing pressure to conform to general IDAP policy: to transfer or discharge patients with drug-positive urines. Ironically, the very program designed to reach out to the poorly motivated and the resistant was now pushing them out into the streets again.

By October 1973 heroin was again being dealt in Altgeld Gardens, and by February 1974 our field-worker identified five part-time dealers, twelve active addicts not in treatment, and five regular heroin experimenters who were not yet addicted. Altgeld Gardens was no longer a heroin-free community. One of the heroin experimenters developed physical dependence in December 1973 and another in February 1974; it was feared that the epidemic might begin to spread again.

In March 1974 the project was reviewed and the decision was made to reinstitute the public health outreach orientation. Aggressive outreach was reintroduced in June, and by August nine of the twelve active heroin addicts and two of the five experimenters were admitted to the program. Continued outreach in September and October resulted in five additional admissions, but this did not eliminate the heroin problem because of the relapse of one patient and the development of physical dependence by two new teenage heroin experimenters.

In late October, members of the Day One Community Advisory

Council approached Spellmon asking, "What is the Drug Abuse Program going to do about the continued heroin dealing?" This led to a new series of community–drug program meetings and in November the council drew up a confidential list of seven resident drug dealers and submitted the list to the Chicago Housing Authority Manager, asking that the individuals named be evicted from their apartments. Approximately one week later Spellmon spoke at the Altgeld Urban Progress Center, condemning public-housing policies that permitted individuals from the inner city to move into Altgeld Gardens and deal drugs. He stated that effective action could be taken against such people only if housing projects were controlled by the residents themselves. In response to this speech, the housing authorities agreed to evict resident drug dealers. The electricity was turned off in an apartment occupied by one of the dealers and there were police raids on the apartments of two other suspected dealers. In December the housing authorities arranged a conference between Spellmon and a representative from the Chicago Police Department to explore possibilities for cooperation. When the officer requested names of suspected drug dealers, Spellmon indicated it would not be possible for a treatment program to give such information. He withdrew from the discussions and this effort at community-police cooperation remained at a stalemate at the close of 1974.

Evaluating the Altgeld Experiment

Documenting the Epidemic

The project was evaluated by analyzing incidence and prevalence trends from July 1970 to December 1974.[5] During this period 105 heroin addicts were identified among Altgeld residents, but for 29 of these cases we have only observational data. These 29 had either moved from the community or were arrested before they could be formally interviewed. Of the 78 addicts on whom complete data were obtained, 57 reported that their first heroin use and onset of withdrawal symptoms (physical dependence) occurred while they were residents of Altgeld Gardens. The remaining 21 had initiated their heroin use and/or their withdrawal symptoms had developed while residing in some other community. Because they were not in the narrow sense products of this neighborhood epidemic, they were not included in our analysis of incidence trends. The mean age for first heroin use among addicts produced in this neighborhood was 20.1 years ($N = 57$, SD = 3.1).

Trends in the annual incidence of first heroin use and onset of withdrawal symptoms are shown in figure 17. Observe that between 1948 and 1966 this community, assuming that our data are relatively complete, produced no more than two new cases per year. In 1967 and 1968, we see increasing incidence of first heroin use, reaching a peak of thirteen new cases in 1969 and then beginning to decline in 1970. By 1972 it had reached zero, with four new cases in 1973. Figure 18 also shows the incidence of onset of withdrawal symptoms following the same general trend, with no new cases in 1972, one in 1973, and three during 1974. In this sample the mean time lag between initial heroin use and onset of withdrawal symptoms was six months (range: 1–60 months).

We earlier described the time lag between initial heroin use and the onset of addiction as an "incubation-like" period. This is illustrated in figures 17 and 18, which show the lag between the period of maximal social contagion (peak of incidence of first heroin use) and the period when the full impact of the epidemic is felt by the community (the subsequent accumulation of large numbers of new heroin addicts).

The data are also interesting when we consider that our research

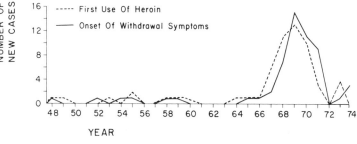

Fig. 17.   Altgeld Gardens: annual trends of first heroin use and onset of withdrawal symptoms

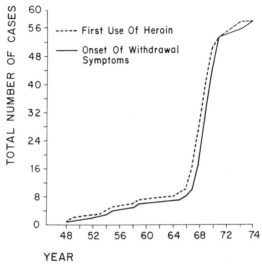

Fig. 18.   Altgeld Gardens: cumulative trends of first heroin
use and onset of withdrawal symptoms

team first became aware of heroin spread in this community
during the spring of 1970. The community itself did not become
visibly alarmed until the spring of 1971, and this concern may
have resulted in part from our intervention activities. We see,
then, another example of a community responding only after it
had accumulated large numbers of new addicts (1971) rather
than during the period of maximal heroin spread (1969).

Impact of Intervention
on Prevalence Trends

The monthly addiction statuses of all 105 addicts appear in figure
19. Despite the frequent movement of individuals from one status
to another, the monthly prevalence remained fairly constant at
about sixty active heroin addicts during the six months of field
investigation in phase 1. During phase 2 of pilot outreach,
however, we observe a slight shift of subjects from active
addiction to active treatment status. During phase 3, the period
of intensive treatment, this shift became clear and dramatic. The
initial reduction in prevalence during phase 3 was due to our

admission of twelve young addicts to the therapeutic community in the summer of 1971. Then when we opened the community treatment facility in November of that year, the shift accelerated.

In our original report of this project,[6] we claimed that we had produced a heroin-free community in July 1972. Five months later, however, another Altgeld resident sought treatment: he had not been known to our field team or counselors because he had not been associating with local heroin users. Although he slept and ate with his family in Altgeld Gardens, his drug-using peer group was located in a center-city neighborhood of Chicago, from which his family had recently moved.

Prevalence of active heroin addicts did eventually reach zero, but we do not suggest that we eliminated addiction in this community. During the month of June 1972, for example, forty-two (71%) of the fifty-nine subjects in treatment were methadone outpatients and seven (12%) were in residential treatment. Only ten (17%) were living in the community free of pharmacological support. Despite the obvious success of the project by the summer of 1972, the addict population of this community was neither cured nor removed. The project had simply provided proper medical care to control the destructive symptoms associated with

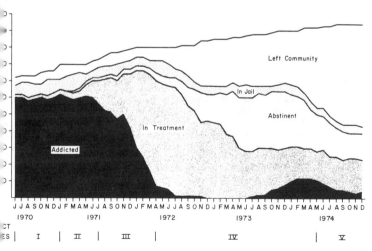

Fig. 19.   Monthly census of Altgeld Gardens addicts

the untreated disorder. It should also be noted that many of the methadone patients were subsequently withdrawn, and by late 1974 only 35% of Altgeld Clinic patients were receiving methadone.

From December 1972 until June 1973, we observed that prevalence of active heroin addicts continued to be zero. This was followed by a gradual increase in prevalence to twelve active addicts during the period February–April 1974, and eleven in May, the month before we reactivated outreach activities. Note that prevalence of active addicts was again reduced to three by December 1974.

Impact on Incidence Trends

We expected the dramatic reduction in prevalence of active addicts would, in turn, reduce the incidence of new cases in several ways. First, as the pool of active heroin addicts was reduced and with it, presumably, the viability and stability of the local heroin distribution system, there should be fewer opportunities for vulnerable individuals to be exposed to active heroin users and to the drug itself. Second, the project shifted the community's sizable population of young heroin addicts into treatment, thereby converting a peer group dynamic that had previously promoted heroin spread into one that discouraged spread. A third factor that was expected to contribute to lower incidence in the future was the increasing ability of adults in this community to recognize drug problems and their decreasing tolerance for addicts who did not seek treatment.

Although the impact of program efforts upon prevalence of active heroin users was immediately observed, the effect upon incidence of new cases was more indirect and additional time was required to assess long-term influence upon these trends. The data in figure 20 suggest an additional problem in measuring program impact on variables where the number of cases is small and where trends show wide fluctuations during different seasons of the year. We see, for example, that trends in first heroin use and onset of withdrawal symptoms, do appear to decline during project phases 1, 2, and 3, but figure 20 shows also that they may already have been on the decline since mid-1969, a full year prior to our initial visit to the area.

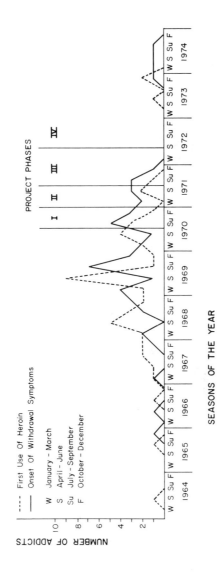

Fig. 20. Quarter annual trends of first heroin use and onset of withdrawal symptoms

We see two possible explanations for the apparent decline of the epidemic prior to our intervention. The first is that the epidemic, having peaked in mid-1969, had simply run its course and was already on the decline when we first visited the area in July 1970. In this case our intervention may merely have accelerated the termination of a self-limited epidemic, or it may have had no effect whatsoever.[7]

A second explanation is that the intervention project did dramatically reverse the course of the epidemic, and incidence of first heroin use in this community was actually higher during the spring of 1970 than during the summer of 1969. But the higher incidence of first heroin use in the spring of 1970 would not appear in figure 20 because we collected data from only those experimenters who eventually required treatment for physical dependence. The intervention project presumably prevented some heroin experimenters from going on to physical dependence, but these cases would be systematically excluded from our analysis. To obtain complete data on incidence of first heroin use, then, an extensive survey of the young people of this community would be required.

This second explanation would argue that successful intervention in an epidemic will always be reflected in a decline in first heroin use trends several months or more before the initiation of control measures, provided that data are collected only on those individuals who develop physical dependence. Given the "incubation" period between first heroin use and the onset of withdrawal symptoms, this is a plausible explanation. On the other hand, how do we explain the lower peak of incidence of onset of withdrawal symptoms observed in the summer of 1970? This was phase 1, when no intervention activity was being carried out. This reduction can only be attributed to the influence of the epidemiological field team during phase 1. Given the small numbers involved, the prevention of only three or four experimenters from becoming physically dependent would have been sufficient to reverse the upward trend.

While neither explanation is entirely satisfactory, the second alternative, namely, that our intervention did significantly alter the course of the epidemic, is more consistent with our earlier study of Chicago's post-World War II heroin epidemic. In that study we also observed that first heroin use trends began to decline approximately one year prior to the launching of a vigorous law enforcement response (see chap. 5). Those trend data were also obtained from addict patients, and again they did not include heroin experimenters who were discouraged by the intervention from continuing their heroin use to the point of developing physical dependence.[8]

Figure 20 also shows the occurrence of four new cases reporting onset of withdrawal symptoms, one during the fall of 1973 and three others in 1974; these data provide indirect support for the notion that the presence of active addicts in a community is associated with heroin spread. The new cases shown in figure 20 occurred when prevalence of active addicts as shown in figure 19 was again on the rise, and presumably heroin was more readily available to experimenters. We are forced to speculate that, had our epidemiological outreach effort remained active during 1973 and early 1974, these four new cases may not have occurred.[9]

Applicability of the Model

The Altgeld experiment demonstrates the ability of an epidemiologically oriented treatment system to identify, document, intervene in, and modify the course of a localized heroin epidemic. The effectiveness of this program technology became more clear in 1973 and 1974, when the outreach public health orientation was relaxed, only to be followed by increasing prevalence and incidence of active heroin addiction. A reactivation of the intervention model was again followed by a decline in prevalence, although at the time of this writing, we had not yet produced a heroin-free community for a second time.

The apparent success of this intervention model is not surprising when one considers that it simply treats heroin addiction as any other communicable disorder. This calls for the provision of effective, convenient, and attractive treatment for all those who have the disorder. It also calls for a public health framework employing well-established epidemiological principles for case finding and for responding rapidly to contain localized epidemics. The model is based upon a notion for which there is considerable evidence—that heroin use is spread by new users. If this group is rapidly involved in treatment, they are not likely to continue spreading the disorder.

Due to the research requirement for extensive data collection and to our own inexperience, the intervention project encountered a number of delays which could not be tolerated as a matter of standard practice. A more rapid implementation of the model, however, has been tested (as described in chap. 6). A modification of our general model has also been tested by another group of researchers,[10] suggesting that it may soon be sufficiently refined for more general application.

Despite these optimistic signs, the future application of this approach will be limited by current methods for treating heroin addiction which, in contrast to those for treating most infectious diseases, are expensive and long term. Unfortunately, any program effort to contain even a relatively small outbreak of heroin addiction will involve the expenditure of many thousands of dollars, and the expenditures are likely to continue for years after the outbreak is contained.

The Altgeld experiment also points to the need for alternative structures for dispensing current treatments. Our response time could have been dramatically reduced had we been able to dispense medication from a local pharmacy, a local hospital, or a mobile treatment unit. In effect, the success of this project depended upon our ability to negotiate and establish an entirely new treatment facility, a process which added six months to phases 2 and 3 of the project.

The Altgeld project is important in still another respect, for the ability of this program to attract adolescent addicts challenges the widespread belief that young drug users are poorly motivated for treatment. Early in the planning stages, Spellmon Young recognized the need to recruit his rehabilitation counselors from among the most influential members of the young group involved. Had he selected older rehabilitation staff, the clinic atmosphere would have been much less attractive to the young people he wished to involve. Treatment systems that are seen by young addicts as punitive or otherwise unattractive could not be expected to achieve similar results. In fact, some punitive and unattractive programs often argue for quarantine and other coercive measures to obtain patients for their facilities.

In the end, the success of the Altgeld project resulted in large part from the strong public health orientation of the program director and his staff. All program activities were organized around the broad public health goal of a heroin-free community. As a concrete example of their public health orientation, the clinical staff of this project relinquished one of the major levers of social control in addiction treatment programs, the expulsion of difficult patients. They quickly recognized that the use of this social control mechanism would undermine the public health commitment to treat all addicts, not just the most cooperative and motivated. They were, in time, able to develop other approaches to influence difficult patients.

During the period in which this public health philosophy was diluted, incidence and prevalence of heroin addiction began to increase again. Unfortunately the public health orientation is not sufficiently widespread in treatment programs. Too many of us feel that the addicts in our community will come to us if they want help and that we need not seek them out.

The Human Issues

A key dimension of the Altgeld project was our need to maintain good relations with community leaders. We must remember that Altgeld Gardens was poor, black, and militant. We entered this community in the summer of 1970 against a setting of explosive racial tensions; the killing of Black Panther leaders on Chicago's West Side, during a raid by the Cook County Sheriff, had been interpreted by many blacks as outright genocide.[11] It was not surprising, then, that in our initial visit to the Altgeld copping area, Dick Parker and I were first introduced to the minister of defense and the minister of information of the local Black Panther party; it was necessary to obtain their sanction to work with the young people of Altgeld. At this meeting we were frankly surprised at their eagerness to have us come into their community. They explained that they were unable to exhort their "brothers" to give up their heroin habits.[12] Although the young addicts would listen with interest to Panther appeals for community responsibility, political rhetoric was simply not strong enough medicine to overcome the pharmacological realities of addiction. Even threats had not worked. When we visited the copping area with the Panther minister of defense, we found the young addicts interested in talking to us because they felt we might be able to help them, but the situation was tense because at the same time they were obviously frightened of revealing their drug habits in front of the Panther leader.

In addition to dealing with the Panthers, we found it necessary to work with the formal community structure. There were no conflicts over the issue of jobs, because from the beginning we had planned to hire community members as staff whenever possible. But there were other problems. Consider just one example: Altgeld Gardens was a public-housing project; most of the adult leaders who formed the Altgeld-Murray Community Council and its Health Committee were women on public assistance. To attend planning conferences they had to pay for baby-sitters and transportation, so several asked us for money to cover these expenses. Initially we were suspicious that they were more interested in personal economic gain than in community service, but we soon recognized the real economic problems that leaders of such desperately poor communities face in simply holding together an organization. We also found the Health Committee was not very interested in assisting us in the purely research aspects of the projects. When planning meetings were held in a location or at a time most convenient for videotaping, community leaders saw this as a service to the university and not of particular interest to the Altgeld community. These issues were finally resolved when we saw the need for, and eventually found, a source for additional funds to pay for baby-sitters, transportation, and participation in research activities.

The crucial human element, of course, was Spellmon Young, the program director and himself a resident of the Altgeld community. In a period of less than one year, he changed his role in the community from that of street addict-dealer to community leader. But these remarkable changes were inevitably accompanied by stress. Because Spellmon was an ex-junkie, representing a state bureaucracy and a university research group, he was initially viewed with suspicion by the community. To resolve this dilemma he decided to build community trust by helping the community to negotiate the most favorable possible arrangements with the state agency and the university. He wished to make it quite clear he would not be used by these outside institutions to exploit the community. This inevitably led to conflicts among Spellmon, the treatment planners, and our research unit, in which we occasionally viewed his alliance with the community as bordering on insubordination.

Spellmon's changing relationship with me was another source of stress. When he was hired in July 1970 as a field-worker, he had a clearly subordinate role. During the course of the following year he gradually became a community leader, a program director, and a peer. Yet he and I continued in our employer-employee relationship. He and I inevitably entered into a series of conflicts which at one point led me to fire him. This event actually was most fortuitous because it permitted us to identify the source of role strain, and the crisis permitted us to renegotiate our relationship as equals. We found a new field-worker to carry out his data collection responsibilities, and Spellmon was rehired as a consultant and fieldwork supervisor, with an appropriate salary increase. The final success of this project was largely due to Spellmon's ability to grow with the changing and complex demands of his position as community leader and program director. We found, then, in Altgeld Gardens as we had at 43d Street, that it was the Spellmons and the Rabbis—with their skills, their charisma and commitment, and their enormous capacities for leadership and growth—who made it possible for us to implement our program planning concepts.

Some Unresolved Issues

Despite the overall success of this experiment, we leave Altgeld Gardens with some unresolved issues, though with many fewer than when we started. For example, we are not able to conclude for certain that the epidemic would not have declined in the absence of intervention. To answer such a question we must conduct future experiments in which intervention communities are paired with control communities which receive only the usual services. A second unresolved methodological issue is the lack of an independent source of case-finding data to determine if there were additional heroin addicts in Altgeld Gardens who were not known to us. Although we had made efforts to obtain access to police drug arrest records for Altgeld residents, this could not be arranged.

We also leave the Altgeld project still not dealing adequately with the heroin experimenter. He is generally poorly motivated for treatment because he does not have clear symptoms of physical dependence. If he is involved in a program, there are no clear and effective treatments for his condition.

Finally, the most serious deficiency in the Altgeld project is our inability to provide jobs for our patients.[13] While not an epidemiological issue, this rehabilitation issue must be adequately resolved if programs employing this model are to produce heroin-free communities.

In the final chapter, specific recommendations will be made to overcome some of the issues not adequately resolved by this project. But first let us briefly review how drug abuse planners in other communities are integrating epidemiological elements into their programs. In this way we might better see how our Chicago work meshes with current trends in the design of addiction control programs.

Epidemiological Elements
in Other Drug Programs

8

Drug abuse epidemiologists are rapidly developing a systematic body of knowledge and techniques. The series of epidemiological intervention experiments we have described is only a
part of that process. Here we wish to move
beyond the limited perspective of one group of
researchers in one community and examine the
role epidemiology is playing in other drug abuse
treatment and control programs. In this review
we will attempt to identify those epidemiological
elements that might eventually become standard
components of addiction treatment and control
systems.

For this analysis we selected four drug abuse
programs which had sufficient epidemiological
orientation and data to provide a basis for
meaningful comparison. We chose two programs from the United States—the U.S. Army
program, and the program of the Washington,
D.C., metropolitan area; we also chose two
programs outside the United States—in England and Japan. Although the Japanese drug
abuse problem has been primarily one of

Portions of this chapter appeared originally in P. H. Hughes,
G. A. Crawford, and W. Dorus, "Epidemiological Elements
of Addiction Control Systems: A Review of Six Programs," in
Developments in the Field of Drug Abuse, ed. E. Senay and
V. Shorty, and Harold Alkane (Cambridge, Mass.: Schenk-
man Publishers, 1975), pp. 239-49.

stimulant abuse, the epidemiological data needs and techniques are, as we shall see, very similar to those of heroin abuse programs. The analysis of these four programs is based upon a review of the available literature rather than on-site inspections.

Vietnam: The Military Model

Since its inception in 1971, the U.S. Army program to control heroin addiction among troops serving in Vietnam has incorporated epidemiological principles.[1] The first principle—identification of all active cases—was made possible by mandatory urine testing of all military personnel. The second principle—treatment of all active cases—is an established epidemiological practice in the prevention of communicable disorders. With the successful treatment of active cases there are presumably fewer individuals in the community to spread the disorder to vulnerable populations. Consistent with this principle, treated cases received follow-up urine testing after they returned to their units. In this way relapse can be quickly detected and these individuals returned to treatment.

Epidemiological approaches were also employed in program evaluation; by monitoring the prevalence of drug-positive urines, the Army could point to a reduction from 4% positive urines among U.S. Vietnam personnel in August 1971 to less than 1% in early 1972.[2]

The military provides an ideal population for the drug abuse epidemiologist and program planner. It is a closed authoritarian social system in which the total population is known and can be manipulated to participate in case-finding and treatment programs. While the military model is not directly applicable to the civilian population, it is presented here as a useful starting point. It offers a clear and relatively uncomplicated model to prepare our thinking for the epidemiological requirements of an open social system which emphasizes personal freedom.

Washington, D.C.: An Epidemiological Surveillance System

One goal of the District of Columbia Narcotics Treatment Administration was to demonstrate the effect of a massive addiction treatment program on urban heroin addiction and addict-related crime. This concern led to an epidemiological surveillance system to analyze the associations between metropolitan crime trends, drug arrest and seizure statistics, treatment program admission data, and deaths due to drug overdosages.

The case-finding procedures for this community-wide monitoring system include questionnaire and urine testing of all patients admitted to the treatment program and of most arrestees awaiting arraignment in the District of Columbia Superior Court Lockup. Cases were also identified by surveying drug problems seen at local health facilities and by reviewing records of drug overdose deaths identified by the District's chief medical examiner. In addition, the system monitored on a monthly basis the number and purity of police drug seizures, the quantities of psychoactive drugs dispensed by local pharmacies, and the cost of drugs on the local illicit market. The monitoring system was based upon information and data that might be readily available to treatment programs in many large urban areas provided that cooperative relationships are maintained with the agencies collecting these data.

The relationships found among these various sets of data suggest the value of monthly monitoring of key epidemiological variables in large urban areas. For example, these data showed a reduction in property crimes during the period of treatment program expansion.[3] The monitoring system also permitted early identification of the peak years of the current epidemic in that city and the beginning of its decline.[4] DuPont and Greene, the architects of this monitoring system, found that the rise and fall of this heroin epidemic paralleled the rise and fall in the purity of heroin available to local addicts and experimenters, the identical pattern we found in Chicago's post–World War II heroin epidemic (see chap. 5). This suggests that such monitoring systems may eventually amass compelling evidence on some universal factors affecting the course of drug epidemics in different settings and points in time.

More recently, the monitoring system was used to document an amphetamine epidemic in the District of Columbia which began in the summer of 1972, peaked in September, and declined rapidly through the final months of that year.[5] The sensitivity of the surveillance system permitted early identification of the

epidemic and a coordinated action response by the drug treatment program, the medical society, and law enforcement agencies. The source of increased amphetamine availability was
traced to the unscrupulous prescribing practices of six physicians; criminal charges were brought against them and the
offending pharmacies. Simultaneously the local medical society
established strict guidelines on the appropriate use of amphetamines and requested manufacturers to restrict their shipments of
the drug to the District. These measures were carried out in the
context of considerable mass media coverage and public concern.
The monitoring system was then able to document the decline of
the epidemic, using such measures as the percentage of amphet-
amine-positive urines among patients and new admissions in the
treatment system and among arrestees, the number of ampheta-
mine-positive results among opiate overdose victims, the number
of amphetamine seizures by police, the quantities of the drug
dispensed by pharmacies, and the rise in price of the drug on the
illicit market.

England: The Medical
Epidemiology Model

Government policy on the treatment of heroin addicts in England, unlike that in the United States, has developed in a setting
relatively free from emotional public debate and political con-
troversy. Physicians have been the major architects through
policy recommendations of the Rolleston Committee in 1926 and
of the Brain Committee in 1960 and 1965.[6] Although British
addicts can be arrested for possession and sale of the drug, the
treatment system throughout the nation has a distinctly medical
rather than punitive orientation. Treatment for drug dependence, as for any health disorder, is available to all who
seek it. It relies primarily upon physician-dispensed care,
including methadone and heroin maintenance and supportive
psychotherapy.

As might be expected, this medical orientation incorporates
epidemiological elements. Case finding is based upon mandatory
reporting of all heroin users identified by physicians and drug
abuse treatment programs; the reporting system serves as a case

registry only and has no punitive effects for the drug user.[7] By using these reports, planners can develop national statistics on the total number of cases identified, the number and characteristics of newly identified cases, and the number of addicts in treatment at any given time. These data were valuable in documenting the increasing number of new heroin users during the mid-1960s and the subsequent decline in new cases during the early 1970s.[8] Spear, who reconstructed the historical events affecting the course of this epidemic,[9] linked much of the increased heroin use to the irresponsible prescribing practices of six physicians. By introducing tighter controls over narcotic prescription practices, diversion of pharmaceutical heroin was dramatically reduced.[10] When we consider that this recent British heroin epidemic produced no more than several thousand new addicts and was in large part physician induced, the usefulness of the strong medical orientation to treatment and epidemiology becomes apparent. The case register appears to be a useful tool, but without an epidemiological field team continuously reaching out to identify new users, it is difficult to determine what proportion of the total addict population has been identified at any given time.

In addition to this rather straightforward approach to case finding and monitoring on a national level, there have been a number of intensive case-finding studies in circumscribed communities.[11] For example, the disease transmission tree technique used in chapter 5 to portray heroin spread in Chicago was originally developed by de Alarcon to study an epidemic in a London suburb.[12] In another study, de Alarcon and Rathod compared the effectiveness of various sources of case-finding data for identifying addicts in circumscribed communities, namely, treatment programs, probation officers, physicians, and other drug users.[13] They found the most effective approach was to obtain the assistance of drug abusing patients to identify other users. More recently, de Alarcon demonstrated the usefulness of monitoring drug abuse trends on the microcommunity level by documenting a sudden but short-lived amphetamine epidemic.[14] The documentation and control of this epidemic bear many similarities to the 1972 amphetamine epidemic in Washington, D.C., described above.

Japan: The Law and Order Model

During World War II Japanese airmen and soldiers were often given amphetamines to increase their fighting spirit. When the war ended, pharmaceutical companies turned to the public to unload their large stockpiles, advertising the drug as a means of restoring energy and a sense of well-being to a people demoralized by military defeat. The use of methamphetamine ampules spread throughout Japan.[15] By 1948 methamphetamine was listed as a dangerous drug, and the following year pharmaceutical companies were warned to suspend production. But the number of abusers continued to increase as the legitimate supply was replaced by black market production. Legislation in 1951 to control smuggling and manufacture again proved ineffective, and it was not until 1955 when there were an estimated 550,000 abusers, 200,000 of whom were said to show some psychotic symptoms, that effective legislation and programs were introduced.[16]

A simultaneous attack was directed at amphetamine supply and demand. Legal supplies of the drug were controlled by strict regulations over manufacture, distribution, and prescription; illicit supplies were controlled by restricting import and manufacture of the ingredients used in black market laboratories and by imposing heavy penalties for smuggling and for illicit manufacture, sale, or possession. Demand for the drug was reduced by aggressive police roundup of amphetamine users, who were then sentenced to prison or committed to mental hospitals. This period of enforced abstinence was followed by close supervision in the community. The introduction of these measures is said to have been followed by a dramatic reduction in prevalence of amphetamine use. Thereafter, heroin addiction, formerly of secondary importance, emerged as the country's most serious drug problem.

By 1963, when effective legislation was introduced, there were an estimated 50,000 heroin users. Control measures were similar to those developed for amphetamine use, but penalties were more severe and physicians were required to report all case contacts with heroin users. These measures, when combined with the systematic breakup of organized criminal elements in the drug distribution system, resulted in rapid control. By 1970 authorities reported with some confidence that there were no active heroin addicts in Japan.[17]

The Japanese approach to addiction control applies several epidemiological principles. The first is effective control of the drug supply; this is very much in the tradition of classical public health epidemiology, which seeks to control the disease-producing agent. The second principle is a vigorous effort to identify all active cases and involve them in treatment, with close follow-up to guard against relapse. While citizen informants and mandatory reporting by physicians do play a role, the police and Department of Health Narcotic Control officers serve as the major case-finding agents.[18]

Japanese police and narcotic control officers are not burdened by complicated arrest procedures. A suspect with a history of drug possession can be arrested upon suspicion of use; he need not actually possess contraband or drugs. If the charge is contested in court, two psychiatrists examine the suspect; if he is found to be addicted, he is sent to prison or to a hospital. Because of relatively unencumbered police practices and high conviction rates, it has been possible to round up large numbers of drug users.[19]

The third epidemiological principle is the pooling of arrest data to permit monitoring of national drug abuse trends. These trend data show a dramatic increase in annual arrests of stimulant users to a peak of 55,661 in 1954, when the effective legislation was passed, followed by a dramatic reduction to 5,233 in 1956 and to 271 in 1958.[20] A less dramatic decline in heroin addict arrests followed the 1963 legislation and was again interpreted as an indicator of the success of the new legislation. Statistics presented in the literature, however, have the usual limitations of arrest data; an unknown number of addicts are arrested more than once, and an unknown number of addicts may not be arrested at all.

This Japanese "law and order" approach to drug addiction appears to be effective in a criminal justice system in which addicts can be arrested upon suspicion and the majority of those arrested receive stiff penalties. It must be noted, however, that these program elements may not have been the only factors contributing to a successful control effort. Certainly, social and economic factors may have also influenced the decline of drug addiction in Japan. At the height of the amphetamine epidemic in 1954, there were two applicants for every job, but by 1962 there was a labor scarcity.

Common Epidemiological Needs and Approaches

Although the four programs just reviewed differ markedly in their legal frameworks, their treatment methods, their socio-cultural settings, and even in the drugs to be controlled, they all employed strikingly similar epidemiological principles. Like our Chicago model, these programs all placed major emphasis upon (1) intensive case-finding efforts to identify and "treat" all active addicts, and (2) the monitoring of incidence, prevalence, and other epidemiological trends to evaluate the impact of treatment and other control measures over time.

Each of the four programs employed special case-finding approaches; there was no naive assumption that the majority of drug users would present themselves to program admission units. For an efficient but authoritarian model, the U.S. Army required compulsory urine testing of all suspected drug users. The Japanese approach was equally unencumbered in permitting police to pick up anyone suspected of drug use for compulsory medical examination. In England, where heroin and methadone maintenance and other forms of medical treatment are available to all addicts free of charge, the programs seem attractive enough to involve the vast majority of addicts without coercion; and because compulsory reporting of addicts identified by English physicians brings no punitive response, the registry there is believed to be rather complete. In Washington, D.C., we find yet another model. Multiple institutional sources are surveyed for case-finding data: drug treatment programs, police and court lockups, coroner, and general medical facilities.

The combined experience of these four programs suggests that, once aggressive case-finding procedures are established and the data are pooled for community-wide or national level monitoring of incidence and prevalence trends, program planning becomes more dynamic and purposeful. The step-by-step modifications of the Japanese control efforts during the early 1950s until an effective program formula was achieved is a case in point. The monitoring of arrest trends permitted Japanese planners to observe the ineffectiveness of early control measures followed by the rather dramatic impact of the effective policies initiated in 1955. Similarly, the sensitive epidemiological monitoring system established in Washington, D.C., demonstrated its value in early identification of an amphetamine epidemic, leading to rapid introduction of effective countermeasures; the effectiveness of these measures was in turn reflected in the monitoring system. We also pointed to the decline in the percentage of drug-positive urines in the U.S. Army in early 1972, and the decline in the number of new addict case reports in England in the late 1960s; in each of those settings the trend data suggested a decreasing drug problem following the introduction of treatment and other control programs.

Unfortunately the four programs reviewed are in no way representative of drug abuse programs in most communities, as the vast majority neglect epidemiological concerns and few have epidemiologists on their staff. The adoption of common epidemiological emphases in the four programs just reviewed, however, does suggest some universality of need and approach. In addition, this brief overview provides a basis in the following chapter for broader and more comprehensive recommendations than would be permissable were we to draw solely upon our Chicago experience for their formulation.

9   The American people and their policymakers have been led to believe that their heroin addiction treatment system, which has now mushroomed to massive and expensive proportions, will act as a more effective system of addiction control than the purely law-enforcement approach that preceded it. But unless this treatment system incorporates epidemiological principles in its design and its evaluation, policymakers will have no way of knowing if the implicit promise has been kept. They will have no basis for judging whether or not these programs have measurably reduced the nation's drug problem.

In the preceding chapters we reviewed our efforts to incorporate epidemiological functions into the Illinois Drug Abuse Program and we reviewed relevant work by others to do this elsewhere. These selected examples suggest that heroin addiction may be both controllable and preventable. Our own work in Chicago argues that concentrated treatment-outreach programs could markedly reduce chronic addiction in communities where it is now endemic. After additional experimentation with both the Chicago and Washington models for early identification and response to local drug epidemics, it seems reasonable to consider developing a national level surveillance and response system, a system which would contain future heroin outbreaks before they reached the massive and destructive proportions of our recent nationwide epidemic.

If it is to meet its public health mandate for effective addiction control, America's drug abuse treatment system must move beyond a service-giving orientation to one that is more dynamic and epidemiologically responsive. To facilitate this shift, a series of recommendations follow which are designed to further develop the epidemiological potential of the current treatment system. While these recommendations are oriented toward national and local program design in the United States, it is hoped that they are generalizable enough to be useful in other settings.

**Program Orientation, Structure,
and Administration**

The major emphases in treatment program development during the past several years have been, quite correctly, to expand treatment services, to improve standards of patient care, and to experiment with a variety of treatment approaches. But now that these goals have been achieved, the challenge has shifted to the question of how that massive treatment system can best be structured to have measurable impact upon the problem of heroin addiction. Epidemiological principles and techniques must be employed to answer this question.

An Epidemiological Orientation
in Treatment Program Design

Few drug abuse treatment systems have integrated epidemiological principles into the design of their programs. The philosophical orientation of most treatment systems is still primarily based on the humanitarian wish to offer medical, psychosocial, or vocational rehabilitation services to those who actively seek them. Treatment systems do not generally assume responsibility for either preventing or controlling serious forms of drug abuse in their respective communities. They generally argue, however, that they do contribute to addiction control to the extent that they are able to convert active addicts into productive citizens. The flaw in this logic is that without epidemiological measures we have no way of knowing whether new heroin users are being recruited as rapidly as well-motivated addicts are being re-habilitated.

The epidemiologically oriented treatment system, in contrast to the service oriented system, defines itself as one of several instruments of addiction control. It evaluates its services primar-ily in terms of their contribution to preventing the number of new cases or reducing the number of untreated chronic cases in the community. Poorly motivated and uncooperative patients are rarely, if ever, discharged, because in all probability they will only return to the community to become active carriers and spreaders of the disorder. With the epidemiological orientation, a treat-ment program supports efforts by other agencies that might have impact on incidence and prevalence of the disorder—for ex-ample, law enforcement efforts to reduce drug availability. For treatment systems to assume this orientation, however, they must build into their programs epidemiological elements that provide an appropriate data base and response system on both the regional and local levels.

Local Monitoring and Outreach Units

There is need for a decentralized system of mobile epidem-iological field teams. The teams would engage in intensive case-finding and outreach activities and would investigate new drug-use patterns and new epidemics. Thus the field team would function as an intelligence gathering arm of the treatment system. To assure its acceptance among drug users in the community, the team should be attached to a local voluntary treatment system, but it would also be responsive to the data collection and research needs of the regional monitoring and planning agency.

Regional Monitoring and
Planning Units

There is a need for centralized pooling of all case reports from drug treatment services in a given region or state. If cases identified by other systems—addict arrestees, and overdose and hepatitis cases—were also included, the data base would be that much more complete. Routine reporting of all cases of heroin and other serious forms of drug dependence would permit regional planners to determine the need and location of treatment facilities and to observe alterations in incidence and prevalence trends in response to new programs, policies, and even unplanned events. Ideally, all treatment programs in a given area would participate so that the regional epidemiology system would serve a function similar to that of a case registry. The state or regional planning agency would then feed data into a national-level case-reporting system to permit monitoring of national drug abuse trends.

To permit the pooling and comparison of these various sources of data, the different reporting systems should collect information on identical core items. Where possible it is desirable for the different agencies to use the same reporting form, and the data management system should include safeguards to protect against the duplicate counting of cases.

A structure for such a regional data system does now exist in the United States in the Client Oriented Data Acquisition Process (CODAP), sponsored by the National Institute of Drug Abuse (NIDA). Under this system demographic and other information is collected on all patients treated in federally funded programs. Safeguards have been established to protect the confidentiality of case records and work is in progress to extend this reporting system to patients in nonfederally supported programs.[1]

National Monitoring System

The current efforts by the National Institute of Drug Abuse to develop a national data collection system to monitor patients in treatment (CODAP) should be supported. Although its primary purpose is to serve as an accountability and management mechanism for federally funded treatment services, it has potential for evolving into a national-level system for monitoring incidence and prevalence trends for serious forms of drug dependence.

Because CODAP was designed primarily as a management tool, it has certain limitations as an epidemiological data gathering system. Nevertheless it does receive reports from over one thousand federally funded treatment facilities, which represent approximately half of the drug dependence treatment services in the country. Data are reported on standardized forms and instructions are issued to describe how they are to be collected, but in practice it is difficult to assure a high level of reliability.

Since the data are collected on patients in treatment, CODAP tends to give us information on the more serious cases of drug dependence. For a more composite picture of the total drug using population, other sources of data are necessary—for example, drug-related arrests, surveys of the general population, and surveys of special groups such as students. Such a framework for obtaining drug use trend information using multiple indicators appears to be developing on the national level. Despite these positive developments toward an effective national monitoring system, the limitations and shortcomings of the various data sources must be carefully considered in interpreting the results of the suggested trends.

Administration and financing

A public health oriented treatment system of the genre suggested by our Chicago experience would assign epidemiological research, planning, and data analysis functions to a central drug abuse planning agency for a state or metropolitan area. Field activities logically would be decentralized and attached to local treatment systems but would still be responsive to central planning and data needs. A flexible financial and administrative structure would be required to permit rapid expansion of treatment services in areas with new heroin outbreaks, with gradual reduction in program size and funding as the need declined. Highly trained epidemiological research and planning personnel would be located in the regional unit, with the field units staffed by experienced but less highly trained personnel, and with temporary employees to help in localized epidemics.

Research, Training, and Demonstration Projects

Research and Training Centers

There is need for several centers of epidemiological expertise attached to the planning and administrative units of large drug treatment programs. A university affiliation would be desirable to strengthen their research and training capability. Such centers are seen as overlooking the monitoring of incidence and prevalence data from treatment programs in the region and exploring other potential sources of epidemiological data for monitoring purposes. They would have mobile epidemiological field teams to explore the role of this element in prevention and control. These centers would serve as training sites for professionals to gain expertise, and they would sponsor research investigations on questions related to the etiology and control of various forms of drug abuse.

Study of Drug Epidemics

Drug abuse epidemics, particularly those involving opiate use, are devastating in their immediate effects, and they leave in their wake large populations of chronic addicts to burden the community for long periods. Because our Chicago experience and the experiences of others reviewed in chapter 8 suggest that the course of these epidemics can be altered by systematic intervention, we must learn more about the natural and programmed events that influence their course. The careful monitoring of these epidemics in multiple settings will in itself contribute significantly to our knowledge, particularly where data can be collected on potentially controllable causal factors such as drug purity and availability and on intervention measures such as treatment and law enforcement activity.

Leon Hunt[2] has recently applied mathematical models and diffusion theory concepts to the study of heroin spread, thereby opening up an entire new dimension in our theoretical understanding of drug epidemics. By analysis of data collected by the de Alarcon disease-transmission-tree technique, Hunt was able to quantify the period during which new heroin users are "contagious" and, on statistical grounds, to question the likelihood that intervention programs can influence the course of localized epidemics. There are many among us who must challenge Hunt's pessimistic conclusion on the basis of other data and experience, and O'Donnell has questioned his conclusion on methodological grounds.[3] Nevertheless, we must recognize Hunt's application of these more sophisticated quantitative techniques to the study of

heroin spread as a welcome contribution.[4] If they are appro-
priately applied to our analyses of epidemiological data, they may
eventually strengthen the scientific basis for our concepts of
etiology, prevention, and control.

Early Intervention Response
to Heroin Epidemics

With improved techniques for monitoring incidence and prevalence trends on both neighborhood and regional levels, new
opportunities will arise to test different strategies for early
identification and control of heroin and other drug abuse epidemics. The four-phase research-intervention model developed
for our Chicago work is one possibility; the model described in
the preceding chapter to control a recent amphetamine epidemic
in Washington, D.C., is another. Because so little work has been
done in this area to date, there is considerable opportunity for
testing a variety of innovative approaches. It is hoped that the
methodological limitations of our own experiments and of the
Washington approach can be overcome; namely, these were
simple before-and-after experiments in single communities. They
did not involve the simultaneous monitoring of control communities with similar drug problems but without special intervention programs.

Addiction Control in Endemic Areas

For many years to come we will need not only a strategy for
controlling new epidemics but also a system for managing the
drug dependent populations produced by past epidemics—the
tens of thousands of chronic addicts in our large cities. We are
likely to find in such areas as Chicago's "old dope neighborhoods" that heroin addiction is endemic and highly resistant to
eradication efforts by treatment programs.[5] These high-vice,
high-crime areas, with their lack of stable community structure,
present an addiction control problem as formidable as the task of
cleaning up the "skid row" neighborhoods of chronic homeless
alcoholics. Elimination of addiction in endemic areas would not
only benefit the addicts directly affected, it would also remove
these permanent sources of illicit heroin, a crucial measure in the
prevention of future epidemics. There is a need for demonstra-

tion projects to test different strategies for eliminating active addiction in such neighborhoods. While these projects would no doubt employ outreach teams and offer attractive, convenient treatment to all addicts in the area, they may also need to develop and test additional program elements.

Further Development of Mobile Epidemiological Teams

The mobile epidemiological team can provide a mechanism to implement current federal plans to pilot test a variety of outreach program models.[6] Through trial and error, our Chicago group evolved a concept of mobile epidemiological teams to give the treatment system "eyes and ears" and therapeutic presence in the community. We found a workable structure based upon ex-addict field-workers who were either patients or rehabilitation counselors in the treatment system and who were known and trusted by addicts in their own neighborhoods. In practice the most competent field-workers had been drug dealers prior to entering treatment. We also found it useful to place our team under the joint supervision of a highly responsible ex-addict and a social scientist trained in field research methods. Both supervisors made visits to the field to observe the workers' performance and to check the reliability of their observations.

Additional experience is needed in selecting and training field-workers and in deciding if it is necessary to hire the ex–drug dealer. More work is required to refine their data collection and intervention procedures and the field concepts used to organize their activities. We do not know the optimal number of field-workers required to halt a localized epidemic. Once a heroin-free community has been produced, what follow-up functions must be performed by field-workers to prevent incidence and prevalence from rising again?

Joint Experiments with Law Enforcement Agencies

Although our own work has been conducted in relative isolation from local law enforcement agencies, there may be opportunities to experiment with collaborative relationships. One obvious example of such a relationship is the model developed for alcoholics in some communities where police are able to pick up and transport problem alcoholics to rehabilitation centers, thereby avoiding the necessity for arrest. Similar procedures could be explored for heroin addicts, providing they did not violate the addicts' civil liberties or interfere unduly with police work. In any such collaborative work with law enforcement agencies, epidemiological and treatment program personnel must establish clear ground rules in order to preserve the confidentiality of information obtained within the therapeutic relationship and to protect the program from being seen by drug users as merely an extension of the law enforcement system.

Conferences and Dissemination
of Information

There is need for national and international level conferences devoted specifically to the role of epidemiology in treatment program design. These conferences would be arenas for the sharing of experience and knowledge. Collaborative international projects might be organized to take advantage of the opportunity to study or intervene in unique drug abuse situations. Furthermore, by reviewing the epidemiological needs of programs in different cultural settings, the universal principles and requirements are more likely to be identified. Considerable groundwork in this area has already been laid,[7] and it will be important to keep up this momentum.

Treatment and Rehabilitation

Improved Treatment and Rehabilitation

Our Chicago experiences demonstrate the need for drug abuse programs to provide attractive and convenient treatment if they are to involve and hold the majority of drug users in any given community. But even beyond this consideration, current treatment modalities are still expensive and require considerable patient motivation and commitment to a long-term process. Clinical researchers and psychopharmacologists require continued support in their efforts to develop more effective, low-cost treatment methods and service delivery systems which will not require inordinate degrees of motivation by patients.

Community Involvement

Inevitably, drug abuse programs will experience the bureaucratic tendency to economize by consolidating treatment services in large centralized facilities. The decentralized neighborhood-staffed services in Chicago and some other cities are certain to come under attack as too expensive. But attractiveness and convenience of treatment appears crucial to effective addiction control, particularly in areas experiencing new outbreaks of heroin use. As our own experience in Altgeld Gardens so clearly demonstrated, basing the treatment program in the neighborhood allows planners to recruit local staff members who can establish rapport with the addicts involved—an advantage in any case, but especially so with new young addicts who may be less motivated for treatment. Moreover, the neighborhood-based facility minimizes time and transportation demands on addicts regularly receiving methadone or other medication.

It is doubtful that the Altgeld Gardens experiment would have been successful without the active participation of the Community Council. The council provided the proper arena to deal with the related problems of public housing, unemployment, and law enforcement. Clearly, community involvement must be a key element in the design of effective addiction control programs and the creation of a healthy and stable community environment.

Jobs

The "1974 Federal Strategy"[8] is to be commended for recognizing the need for basic education, vocational counseling, training, and job placement as a priority area of program development if drug abuse rehabilitation efforts are to be successful. One of the major obstacles to our effort to produce a heroin-free community in Altgeld Gardens was the treatment program's inability to place patients in jobs or job training programs. Extensive efforts by programs in other cities to integrate patients into existing job training and placement agencies have been equally discouraging.[9] While the thought of establishing special job training facilities for ex-drug addicts is not appealing either from the economic or the administrative standpoint, there may be no other alternative. We need carefully evaluated and innovative demonstration projects in this field.

The Heroin Experimenter
and Polydrug User

Because of the important place of the polydrug-using friendship group and the heroin experimenter in the early stage of a heroin epidemic, we need more effective case-finding, treatment, and intervention approaches for these vulnerable populations. This high-risk group of young people is difficult to identify and study, and we do not yet know what proportion are likely to become heroin addicts.

A Plea for the Experimental Approach

Our experience in implementing epidemiologically oriented demonstration programs in Chicago neighborhoods suggests that strong leadership and political will would be necessary to implement the foregoing principles on a state-wide or national level. Our work in Chicago was made possible through the fortuitous joining of political and university leadership to provide the needed resources and to recruit the technical level professionals for program implementation. Our work was also carried out at a time of program expansion and availability of financial resources for experimentation with innovative approaches. However, at the time of this writing, federal, state and local drug abuse programs are becoming increasingly entrenched in rigid bureaucracies. As they experience budgetary difficulties due to current economic restrictions, opportunities to apply the proposals outlined in this chapter may for the immediate future be limited. For this reason it will be important to continue federal support of epidemiologically oriented experimental intervention programs until the practical and technical aspects of these community addiction control efforts are worked through.

For too long, solutions to the drug addiction problem have been based upon highly emotional or ideological debate. Fortunately recent developments in the drug field in America have been increasingly based upon findings of clinical research and program evaluation. We are approaching an era in which we should be able to design and compare a whole range of different approaches to drug addiction prevention and control. Improving current models by systematic experimentation will make the road longer but, in the end, more certain.

Notes

Preface

1 Although the term "patient" is used, approximately two-thirds were federal prisoners. Many of the remaining third were referred by state and local courts as a condition of probation. At that time the Fort Worth hospital offered treatment services to addicts residing west of the Mississippi River, and the Lexington, Kentucky, hospital served addicts to the east.

2 P. H. Hughes, "Patients as Therapeutic Agents," in *Rehabilitation of the Narcotic Addict,* ed. Saul Sells, Vocational Rehabilitation Administration (Washington, D.C.: Government Printing Office, 1967):91-95; P. H. Hughes; C. M. Floyd; G. Norris; and G. Silva, "Organizing the Therapeutic Potential of an Addict Prisoner Community," *International Journal of the Addictions* 5, no. 2 (1970): 205-23.

3 D. Casriel, *So Fair A House: The Story of Synanon* (New York: Prentice-Hall, Inc., 1966); D. Casriel and G. Amen, *Daytop: Three Addicts and Their Case* (New York: Hill & Wang, 1971).

Chapter 1

1 "Nodding" is the characteristic slow lowering of the head and simultaneous closing of the eyes, followed immediately by the sudden raising of the head and reopening of eyes after addicts have ingested opiates, including heroin. Nodding addicts give the impression of being about to fall asleep but are in fact quite alert.

2 L. Yablonsky, *Synanon: the Tunnel Back* (Baltimore: Penguin Books, 1965); Casriel, *So Fair a House.*

3 Casriel and Amen, *Daytop,* B. Sugarman, *Daytop Village: A Therapeutic Community* (Toronto: Holt, Rinehart & Winston, 1974).

4 E. Ramirez, *Annual Report* (Rio Pedras, P.R.: Addiction Research Center, 1963-64).

5 Since 1968, we have seen more systematic data on the effectiveness of the therapeutic community approach. Of 337 admissions to Illinois Drug Abuse Program therapeutic communities between mid-1968 and mid-1970, 260 (77%) had dropped out by December 1972. Forty-nine (14%) had graduated, were working, and were drug free by December 1972, and an additional 18 (5%) were judged to be ready for graduate status in the near future. The therapeutic community remains an important treatment approach, but for perhaps only a quarter or a third of the addict population, because of a high drop-out rate and because many heroin addicts assigned to therapeutic community programs never return after the intense confrontation during the screening interviews (see E. C. Senay, et al., "IDAP: Five Year Results," *Proceedings of the Fifth National Conference on Methadone Treatment* [New York: National Association for Prevention of Addiction to Narcotics, 1973], p. 1459). The New York City experience is similar, with 37% of admissions to twelve therapeutic communities remaining after six months and 24% after twelve months. See S. Amari and C. Winick, "A Comparative Analysis of 24 Therapeutic Communities" (Bethesda, Md.: Systems Sciences, Inc.), as reviewed in "Special Report" by D. Zimmerman, *The Journal* Toronto: Addiction Research Foundation, pp. 1, 4, 5, June 1, 1974.

6 It is presently estimated that two years are required to rehabilitate the typical therapeutic community resident. In Chicago, the cost of maintaining one resident was $18.87 per day in 1974, or $6,900 per year. McGlothlin's studies on cost effectiveness estimated $4,000 per patient year in therapeutic communities with minimal professional staff (see W. H. McGlothlin, V. C. Tabbush, C. D. Chambers, and K. Jamison,

Alternative Approaches to Opiate Addiction Control: Costs, Benefits and Potential [Washington, D.C.: U.S. Bureau of Narcotics and Dangerous Drugs, June 1972], pp. 39–40). The cost per patient year in Oddyssey House in New York City, with somewhat more professional supervision, is $6,833 (see Amari and Winick, "A Comparative Analysis").

7   V. P. Dole, M. E. Nyswander, and A. Warner, "Successful Treatment of 750 Criminal Addicts," *Journal of American Medical Association* 206 (1968): 2708–11.

8   In methadone programs the cost per patient year during the 1960s ranged from $500 to $2,750 and averaged about $1,500 (see McGlothlin et al., *Alternative Approaches to Opiate Addiction Control*. Since that time the U.S. Food and Drug Administration has required increased medical supervision, so that costs have increased.

9   Recent evidence suggests that at least one-fourth of the patients doing well on methadone might be successfully withdrawn. Lowinson and Langrod selected 228 chronic addicts with good adjustment in methadone treatment and found 28% were withdrawn as outpatients and 70% of these were abstinent three months later; another 14% returned to methadone (see J. H. Lowinson and J. Langrod, "Detoxification of Long-Term Methadone Patients," *Proceedings of the Fifth National Conference on Methadone Treatment* [New York: National Association for the Prevention of Addiction to Narcotics, 1973], pp. 256–61). Cushman and Dole attempted to withdraw forty-eight well-adjusted patients who had been in methadone treatment for less than eight months. They found 37% achieved abstinence and continued to be abstinent nine months later. An additional 19% achieved abstinence on a second attempt and remained abstinent when seen five months later. The remaining 44% did not achieve abstinence (P. Cushman and V. P. Dole, "Detoxification of Well Rehabilitated Methadone Maintained Patients," from above *Proceedings*, pp. 262–69).

10   J. H. Jaffe, E. C. Senay, C. R. Schuster, P. R. Renault,

B. Smith, and S. Dimenza, "Methyl Acetate versus Methadone: A Double-Blind Study in Heroin Users," *Journal of the American Medical Association* 222 (1972): 437–42.

11 M. C. Braude, L. S. Harris, E. L. May, J. P. Smith, and J. E. Villarreal, *Narcotic Antagonists* (New York: Raven Press, 1973); R. B. Resnick, J. Volavka, A. M. Freedman, and M. Thomas, "Studies of EN 1639A (Naltrexone): A New Narcotic Antagonist," *American Journal of Psychiatry* 131, no. 6 (1974): 646–50.

12 H. Halbach, "Pharmacological Approaches to the Treatment of Morphine-Type Dependence," *International Journal of Clinical Pharmacology* 12, nos. 1–2 (1975): 6–12.

13 R. M. Glasscote et al., "Illinois Drug Abuse Program," in *The Treatment of Drug Abuse* (Washington, D.C.: American Psychiatric Association, 1972), pp. 127–52.

14 P. H. Hughes, J. Chappel, E. C. Senay, and J. H. Jaffe, "Developing In-Patient Services for Community Based Treatment of Narcotic Addiction," *Archives of General Psychiatry* 25, no. 3 (1971): 278–83.

15 Senay et al. "IDAP: Five Year Results."

16 R. de Alarcon, "The Spread of Heroin Abuse in a Community," *Bulletin on Narcotics* 21 (1969): 17–22; A. Kosviner, M. Mitcheson, A. Ogborn, K. Myers, G. Stimson, J. Zacune, and G. Edwards, "Heroin Use in a Provincial Town," *Lancet* 1 (1968): 1189–92.

Chapter 2

1 Preble and Casey and Finestone tended to employ interviews and other formal data collection techniques, while Feldman and Polsky preferred participant observer techniques for their studies (See E. Preble and J. J. Casey, "Taking Care of Business: The Heroin User's Life on the Street," *International Journal of the Addictions* 4 [1969]: 1–24; H. Finestone, "Cats, Kicks and Color," *Social Problems* 5 [July 1957]: 3–13; H. W. Feldman, *Street Status and*

the Drug Researcher: Issues in Participant Observations [Washington, D.C.: Drug Abuse Council, 1974]; and N. Polsky, *Hustlers, Beats and Others* [Chicago: Aldine Publishing Co., 1967]).

2   W. B. Miller, "The Impact of a 'Total-Community' Delinquency Control Project," *Social Problems* 10 (1962): 168–91; P. Crawford, D. I. Malamud, and J. R. Dumpson, *Working with Teenage Gangs* (New York: Welfare Council of New York City, 1950), pp. 21–32, 34–35, 37–38.

3   In 1968–69 Chicago had 12,000 uniformed police and detectives, according to the Public Information Department, Chicago Police Department.

4   P. H. Hughes, R. Parker, and E. L. Senay, "Addicts, Police and the Neighborhood Social System," *American Journal of Orthopsychiatry* 44, no. 1 (1974): 129–41.

5   G. W. Anderson, M. G. Arstein, and R. N. Lester, *Communicable Disease Control* (New York: Macmillan Co., 1962); G. W. Anderson, *Syphilis and Society: Problems of Control in the United States, 1919–1964*, Health Information Foundation Research Series, vol. 22 (Chicago: University of Chicago Press, 1965).

6   The names of our initial four field-workers have been changed to protect their anonymity.

7   Ironically, this man later became a highly successful and respected director of a large, independent drug addiction treatment program in Chicago. His initial difficulties at IDAP were part of the early adjustment problems that addicts have in shifting from the street to straight life.

8   While addicts frequently refer to the dealer as "the Man," this term is used in the American black community to refer to anyone with power or prestige, such as a policeman or a successful entertainer.

9   Epidemiology can be defined as the study of the distribution and the determinants of a condition in populations. Examples of studies of the distribution of drug abuse or drug abuse problems include addict case registers, drug use surveys, hepatitis and death statistics, treatment program admission, and police

arrest statistics. Many studies of the psychosocial characteristics of drug users and efforts to clarify the causes of drug use could also be classified as epidemiological research. Epidemiological studies in the drug abuse field are generally carried out to provide information for planning and evaluating prevention and control programs (see WHO Expert Committee on Drug Dependence, Nineteenth Report, *World Health Organization Technical Report Series*, no. 526 [Geneva: World Health Organization, 1973]).

10 Incidence can be defined as the frequency or the rate of occurrence of a condition in a population. It is a measure of new cases of a disorder, identified by health and other reporting agencies. For health conditions that come to medical attention early in their course, statistics on the incidence of new cases are useful for early identification and for monitoring the spread of the condition. In the case of heroin addiction, however, it may take six months to a year for new heroin users to become physically dependent, and additional months or years may pass before they seek treatment or are arrested. Treatment program incidence data are therefore not sufficiently sensitive for early identification and monitoring of new epidemics. In order to obtain more sensitive information on the actual spread of heroin use, our research team and others have collected retrospective data from already identified users on the dates of first heroin use and onset of withdrawal symptoms. When these trends are presented as in this chapter, they must be distinguished from incidence of new cases identified by health agencies.

11 The Federal Bureau of Narcotics (FBN) was for many years the national law enforcement agency for the control of illicit narcotics. In the early 1970s it was renamed the Bureau of Narcotic and Dangerous Drugs (BNDD) and its mandate was broadened to include enforcement of federal laws controlling "dangerous drugs" such as amphetamines, barbiturates, and LSD. In 1973 the BNDD was incorporated into the Drug Enforcement Agency (DEA) which concentrated all federal drug enforcement and intel-

ligence resources in the Department of Justice. At different points in the telling of our story, then, the text may refer to the FBN, the BNDD, or the DEA, depending upon which of these agencies was operational at the time.

12   The Chicago office of the BNDD permitted Noel Barker confidential access to their case files, so it was not necessary for us to reveal our list of names to the bureau.

13   We must recognize, of course, that Rabbi might not have known every addict in the neighborhood; for the purposes of this particular study, however, we made the assumption that he did.

14   Information obtained during a personal visit to the Mobilization for Youth on New York City's lower East Side during the fall of 1966.

Chapter 3

1   Hughes et al., "Organizing the Therapeutic Potential," (preface, n. 2 above).

2   J. Larner and J. Tefferteller, *The Addict in the Street* (New York: Grove Press, 1964).

3   J. Mills, *The Panic in Needle Park* (London: Sphere Books, 1971).

4   Finestone, "Cats, Kicks and Color" (chap. 2, n. 1 above).

5   R. A. Cloward and L. E. Ohlin, *Delinquency and Opportunity* (New York: Free Press, 1960).

6   A. G. Sutter, "The World of the Righteous Dope Fiend," *Issues in Criminology* 2, no. 2 (1966): 177–222; see also Sutter's "Phases of a Ghetto Career," in *The Dream Sellers,* ed. R. H. Blum (San Francisco: Jossey-Bass, 1972), pp. 201–12. In this later study Sutter traces the developmental history of the righteous dope fiend from the stage of bold and daring children, to "wanting to be the baddest"; then in adolescence the imperative to display masculine aggression and prowess becomes so overwhelming that many sidestep the inevitable violence by turning to drugs. He suggests that those who are sufficiently

qualified to play the cold game of dealing can simultaneously make a good living and derive a ghetto sense of manhood.

7   H. Feldman, "Street Status and Drug Users," *Society* (1973), pp. 32–38; see also Feldman, "Ideological Supports to Becoming and Remaining a Heroin Addict," *Journal of Health and Social Behavior* 9, no. 2 (1968): 131–39, in which the author describes the socialization of young heroin users into New York City's addict subculture.

8   M. Agar, *Ripping and Running: A Formal Ethnography of Urban Heroin Addicts* (New York: Seminar Press, 1973).

9   L. Gould, A. Walker, L. Crane, and C. Lidz, *Connections: Notes from the Heroin World* (New Haven: Yale University Press, 1974).

10 Preble and Casey, "Taking Care of Business" (chap. 2, n. 1 above).

11 Hughes et al., "Organizing the Therapeutic Potential" (pref., n. 2 above); H. A. Wilmer, "The Role of the Rat in the Prison," *Federal Probation* 29 (1965): 44–49.

12 Narcotic enforcement officers and some ex-addicts have the impression that "informing" among young addicts is less common perhaps because of the importance of peer group norms for adolescents. But it is also true that young addicts frequently have not suffered the misfortune of extended periods in prison, and when they are convicted they are frequently given more lenient sentences because of their youth and lack of long arrest records.

13 B. Dai, *Opium Addiction in Chicago* (Shanghai: Commercial Press Ltd., 1937).

Chapter 4

1   Prevalence can be defined as the frequency or the rate at which a condition exists in a population. Point prevalence refers to the frequency or rate of a condition at a designated point in time, for example, June 30, 1970. Period prevalence refers to the frequency or

rate of a condition known to exist during a specified time period, such as the month of June 1970. In this and later chapters we will generally refer to period prevalence and will use frequencies rather than rates. For example, forty-five active heroin users recorded during the month of June in a particular target neighborhood. In practice, prevalence is used in the sense of *extent* of a condition or disorder because it includes both new and chronic cases.

2   Ideally one would prefer objective criteria for case definition, such as positive urine test for opiates or personal observation of heroin injection, fresh needle marks, withdrawal signs, or nodding. While such criteria were not established in this study, the reader will note later in this chapter that we conducted home visits and admitted to treatment a sample of 43d Street subjects. All of those interviewed and admitted provided sufficient evidence of active heroin addiction on the basis of one or more of the above criteria.

3   During 1969 and 1970, the offer of an easy route into IDAP was an incentive for participation in research because treatment services were still limited. Addicts applying for treatment by the usual procedures were required to wait three months or more for admission.

4   In the black and Puerto Rican copping areas, control groups were selected in the following manner: all monitored addicts were paired on the basis of their functional role in the heroin distribution system (dealer, hustler, worker) and whether or not they had completed the survey card. One member of each pair was randomly selected for outreach; the other was assigned to a control group. Because the major purpose of the project was to determine the treatability of representative populations of street addicts, the relative proportions of dealers, hustlers, and workers within the outreach and control samples were selected to approximate their representation in the mid-May census. No attempts were made to contact control subjects either by letter or by field-worker. The field-workers were instructed, when approached by control subjects, to explain that they had not been selected for the project but could receive treatment

through regular channels. To be admitted, then, they were required to visit the centralized intake unit on their own initiative. Their applications were treated in the routine manner: their names were placed on the admission list which at the time still required a three-month waiting period. Those in the outreach group who had indicated an address on the survey cards were sent letters informing them of their selection. Because a third of the sample had refused to complete survey cards, they could be contacted only through the field-workers. Both outreach groups were informed that they would be admitted any Monday or Tuesday during the month of June 1971 if they presented the letter at the intake unit located at a short distance from all three copping areas. They were instructed to contact our research unit to make other arrangements if unable to report on the specified days.

Chapter 5

1   For a general definition of incidence, see chap. 2, n. 10.
2   I. Chein, D. Ferard, R. Lee, and E. Rosenfeld, *The Road to H.* (New York; Basic Books, 1964).
3   The exception to this statement is in military psychiatry, where mental health interventions have contributed to reduced incidence of psychiatric casualties.
4   In early 1969, I had the opportunity to meet several times with Professor Henry McKay of the Institute of Juvenile Research, in Chicago, to discuss our research progress and to take advantage of his decades of experience with criminological research in the city. During one of these meetings he showed me the original data collected by Sol Kobrin and Harold Finestone, during their study of young Chicago heroin addicts in the early 1950s. Interestingly, the publication (reference follows) resulting from this study did not mention the term "epidemic." Yet the notion of a drug abuse epidemic must have been discussed, because Professor McKay specifically used the term

in our initial conversation. This was somewhat of a surprise because we had not been thinking of heroin addiction as an epidemic disorder, and here was an eminent social scientist feeling very comfortable in his use of this public health concept. Later, in 1970, I had the opportunity to serve on a national drug abuse program evaluation committee with Professors Finestone and Kobrin. These meetings gave me a chance to review their experience with the young addicts involved in this epidemic and to benefit from their insights into some of the causes and the community dynamics. I also benefited from their reactions to early drafts of our paper reconstructing the course of this epidemic. See S. Kobrin and H. Finestone, "Drug Addiction among Young Persons in Chicago," in *Gang Delinquency and Delinquent Subcultures,* ed. J. F. Short (New York: Harper & Row, 1965), pp. 110-30.

5 Dai, *Opium Addiction in Chicago* (chap. 3, n. 13 above).

6 "Polydrug" is a contemporary term which means "many drugs." It is used interchangeably with "multiple drug."

7 Finestone, "Cats, Kicks and Colors" (chap. 2, n. 1 above).

8 A. Abrams, J. H. Gagnon, and J. J. Levin, "Psychosocial Aspects of Addiction," *American Journal of Public Health* 58 (1968): 2142-55.

9 Kobrin and Finestone, "Drug Addiction among Young Persons in Chicago"; see also Chicago Police Department annual reports, 1931-58.

10 The arrest data presented here were obtained from annual statistical reports of the Chicago Police Department from 1931 through 1958. Unfortunately these data include arrests not only for heroin and other hard narcotics but also for the soft drugs such as marijuana. Apparently no reports were issued between 1959 and 1963.

11 One could just as readily use the six to twelve month lag period between initial heroin use and onset of physical dependence to argue that the police offensive

did reduce the incidence of new cases. For example, effective police pressure during 1951 would conceivably have discouraged heroin users who had first used in 1950 from becoming addicts in 1951. Using this logic, the year of peak incidence of first heroin use may have actually been 1950, but because many of these new users were prevented by the police activity from becoming fully addicted, they would not show up on our incidence curve. Our year of first heroin use data was developed from those who had become physically dependent and sought treatment many years later. We had no way of obtaining year of first heroin use data from heroin experimenters who never became addicted because it is unlikely that they would have sought treatment. Had we collected data on year of onset of physical dependence, we would no doubt have seen an epidemic peak in 1950; this would suggest the decline observed in 1951 was indeed the direct result of police activity. In chapter 7 we will deal with this same methodological issue again when we evaluate the impact of a medical intervention project on local incidence trends.

12   Judges' minutes were examined on randomly selected days in every fourth year from 1940 through 1960. The year 1950 was also included. We calculated the mean duration of sentences given to drug violators for these years: these are presented in figure 9. Unfortunately, judges' minutes did not distinguish between violations for marijuana, cocaine, and hard narcotics, and the data did not permit us to determine the percentage of convictions for narcotics offenses. Furthermore, the subtleties of plea bargaining precluded an analysis of charges, since prosecutors tend to reduce charges after the passage of harsh legislation in order to obtain more convictions.

13   R. L. McFarland and W. A. Hall, "A Survey of One Hundred Suspected Drug Addicts," *Journal of Criminal Law, Criminology, and Police Science* 44 (1953): 308-19; A. Abrams, D. Roth, and B. Boshes, "Group Therapy with Narcotic Addicts: Method and Evaluation," *Group Psychotherapy* 11 (1958): 244-56.

14   These early programs were ineffective because they

lacked the mainstays of our current treatment technology—namely, urine testing, methadone maintenance, and therapeutic communities.

15   Of Chicago's various newspapers, only the *Chicago Tribune* was available on microfilm for the period of interest. For the years 1945–54, twelve issues per year were read in their entirety for drug news or comment. Issues were selected from the first Monday, Tuesday, and Saturday of March, June, September, and December. The number of articles, column inches, and location and content of articles were analyzed; this is shown in figure 10.

16   *Chicago Tribune,* September 4, 1954, p. 16.

17   Preble and Casey, "Taking Care of Business" (chap. 2, n. 1 above).

18   P. Zimmering, J. Toolan, R. Safrin, and S. B. Wortis, "Heroin Addiction in Adolescent Boys," *Journal of Nervous and Mental Disease* 114 (1951): 19–34.

19   For each of the years between 1943 and 1970, the first ten case records containing heroin laboratory analyses were selected. In many case records, two or more heroin samples were obtained for evidence, so that the number of samples used to calculate average percentage of heroin for most years exceeded ten. Regrettably, ten heroin analyses per year were not available for the period 1944–47. Case records suggest that federal enforcement efforts during these years were largely directed at controlling illegal distribution of proprietary and prescription drugs.

Chapter 6

1   The overall sample ($N=45$) consisted of eighteen whites (six addict-experimenter-nonuser triads), twenty-one blacks (seven triads), and six Latinos (two triads), who ranged in age from eighteen to twenty-nine years. Thirty-six subjects were males, nine were females. White subjects were drawn primarily from middle-class suburban areas to the northwest and west of Chicago, blacks and Latinos from lower-class ghetto areas on the city's South and West Sides.

Fifteen of the twenty-one blacks were residents of one community, Altgeld Gardens, a low-income housing project on Chicago's far South Side.

2 The author gratefully acknowledges the contributions of Dr. Gail Crawford who conducted the interviews and shouldered the major responsibility for executing this project, and of Dr. Eric Schaps who helped develop the research design.

3 De Alarcon, "The Spread of Heroin Abuse in a Community" (chap. 1, n. 16 above).

4 For purposes of compiling population statistics in Chicago, the city has been divided into seventy-six community areas. These areas are not equal in population size, but each has a community name, such as Lawndale, South Shore, etc (see E. M. Kitagawa and K. E. Taeuber, eds., *Local Community Fact Book, Chicago Metropolitan Area 1960* [Chicago: Chicago Community Inventory, University of Chicago, 1967]).

5 R. de Alarcon and N. H. Rathod, "Prevalence and Early Detection of Heroin Abuse," *British Medical Journal* 2 (1968): 549–53; Kosviner et al., "Heroin Use in a Provincial Town" (chap. 1, n. 16 above).

6 In November 1973, approximately twenty months after completion of the initial intervention experiment, the original patient contact was rehired as a field-worker to assist Gail Crawford in arranging follow-up interviews with the original South Shore outreach subjects and in visiting drug-user meeting places.

Chapter 7

1 The reader may recall that our early intervention projects were not as successful as we had hoped because we were able to admit only a limited number of outreach subjects and within specified time periods. We also found that some outreach subjects did not respond because they found their particular treatment unit inconvenient, or in other ways unattractive. Recall, for example, how Mexican-American outreach subjects felt they were not welcome and saw the program as primarily serving black addicts because of the large number of black staff: at that early stage of

development IDAP had only one Mexican-American counselor. In the Altgeld experiment Dr. Senay was in a position to give full IDAP support to correct these early deficiencies in our model. We were promised adequate resources to provide "attractive and convenient treatment services to all addicts in the Altgeld community."

2 Another major deficiency in our earlier outreach projects was that they had been limited to intensive short-term efforts. When we later evaluated their impact, we found copping area prevalence had returned to preintervention levels in endemic neighborhoods (see chap. 4), and we found heroin continued to spread in epidemic neighborhoods (chap. 6). For these reasons "persistent outreach" was added as a core feature of our evolving program model.

3 The author wishes to thank the members of the Altgeld-Murray Community Council for their continuous support of this project and in particular Irene Darling, Martha Kindred, Gladys Robinson, and Ruth Winters of the Council's Health Advisory Committee. I also wish to thank the Chicago Housing Authority, in particular Elton Barrett for making convenient facilities available for the treatment program and for other forms of support.

4 When we declared Altgeld Gardens a community free of active heroin addicts in July 1972, we were not aware of one additional addict who surfaced to seek treatment five months later. This case-finding issue will be discussed in greater detail later in this chapter.

5 The primary source of incidence and prevalence data was a self-administered questionnaire completed by each addict upon admission to treatment. In addition to dates of first heroin use and onset of withdrawal symptoms, the questionnaire asked for a monthly history of the subject's addiction status from January 1970 until his entry into treatment. Questionnaire responses were checked for accuracy by an ex-addict counselor or field-worker who generally was a long-term acquaintance of the respondent. While in treatment, the current addiction status of the patient was assessed by a questionnaire given at the end of each month. If he dropped out of treatment, the monthly

status report was completed by a staff member on the basis of information available. An additional source of incidence and prevalence data was the logbook maintained by the epidemiological field-worker assigned to the neighborhood. The log was a weekly census of all active heroin addicts known to him and residing in that geographical area. In addition to their drug use, treatment, and arrest statuses, he described each addict's role and functions in the local heroin subculture.

6 P. H. Hughes, E. C. Senay, and R. Parker, "The Medical Management of a Heroin Epidemic," *Archives of General Psychiatry* 27, no. 5 (1972): 585–91.

7 The IDAP patient data show 1969 as the peak year of initial heroin use during Chicago's recent epidemic, so one could argue that Altgeld Gardens trends merely reflected the citywide pattern. See Leon Hunt's excellent analysis of peak year of first heroin use trends in other American cities affected by this nationwide epidemic (L. G. Hunt, *Recent Spread of Heroin Use in the United States: Unanswered Questions* [Washington, D.C.: Drug Abuse Council, 1974]).

8 de Alarcon offered another explanation when he observed the incidence of new admissions to drug treatment centers leveling off prior to the introduction of control measures in England. He suggested the epidemic declined because the susceptible population had been exposed (see R. de Alarcon, "Lessons from the Recent British Drug Outbreak," in *Anglo-American Conference on Drug Abuse Proceedings* [London: Royal Society of Medicine, 1973], pp. 49–54).

9 While analyzing data for a five-year followup of this project, two additional new Altgeld patients reported onset of withdrawal symptoms in 1974. Although these data became available too late to be included in the figures for this chapter, they increase to six the number of new cases in the new outbreak of heroin spread.

10 L. Judd, D. A. Deitch, and E. E. de Giacomo, "The Elimination of a Heroin 'Copping Zone': A Preliminary Report of a Treatment Strategy," *Proceed-*

ings of the Fourth National Conference on Methadone Treatment (New York: National Association for Prevention of Addiction to Narcotics, 1972), pp. 85-88.

11   R. Wilkins and R. Clark, *Search and Destroy: A Report by the Commission of Inquiry into the Black Panthers and the Police* (New York: Metropolitan Applied Research Center, 1973).

12   During my work as a volunteer physician at the Black Panther Free Medical Clinic in Lawndale, I had heard some Panthers express their suspicion that methadone treatment—which keeps the addict in a pharmacologically dependent state—might be used as just another form of white majority oppression of black people. For this reason, the Black Panther invitation for IDAP to enter Altgeld was unexpected.

13   For an overview of the problem of job training and placement for addict patients, we recommend Hugh Ward's *Employment and Addiction: Overview of Issues* (Washington, D.C.: Drug Abuse Council, 1973).

Chapter 8

1   H. L. Ruben, "A Review of the First Year's Experience in the U.S. Army Alcohol and Drug Abuse Program," *American Journal of Public Health* 64, no. 10 (1974): 999-1001; J. E. Flaherty, *Army Drug Abuse Program: A Future Model?* (Washington, D.C.: Drug Abuse Council, 1973).

2   R. S. Wilbur, statement before Committee on Government Operations, House of Representatives, 93d Congress, *Progress and Status of the Drug and Alcohol Abuse Programs of the Department of Defense and the Armed Services,* June 28, 1973.

3   R. L. DuPont, "Heroin Addiction Treatment and Crime Reduction," *American Journal of Psychiatry* 128 (1972): 856-60.

4   R. L. DuPont, "Profile of a Heroin Addiction Epidemic," *New England Journal of Medicine* 285 (1971): 320-24; R. L. DuPont and M. H. Greene, "The Dynamics of a Heroin Epidemic," *Science* 181 (1973): 716-22; M. H. Greene and R. L. DuPont,

"Heroin Addiction Trends," *American Journal of Psychiatry* 131, no. 5 (1974): 545-50.

5   M. H. Greene and R. L. DuPont, "Amphetamines in the District of Columbia," *Journal of the American Medical Association* 226, no. 12 (1973): 1437-40.

6   E. Josephson, "The British Response to Drug Abuse," in *Drug Use in America: Problem in Perspective,* Technical Papers of the Second Report of the National Commission on Marijuana and Drug Abuse, Appendix 4, Treatment and Rehabilitation (Washington, D.C.: Government Printing Office, 1973, pp. 176-97).

7   F. B. Glaser and J. C. Ball, "The British Narcotic 'Register' in 1970: A Factual Review," *Journal of the American Medical Association* 216, no. 7 (1971): 1177-82.

8   T. H. Bewley, "The Treatment of Opiate Addicts in the United Kingdom (1968-1971)" (presented at the Fifth World Congress of Psychiatry, Mexico City, 1971).

9   H. B. Spear, "The Growth of Heroin Addiction in the United Kingdom," *British Journal of Addiction* 64 (1969): 245-55.

10 Unlike the United States, where heroin is banned from medical practice, in England it is prescribed by physicians who feel it has advantages over other narcotic drugs for certain conditions, such as severe pain in terminal cancer.

11 Kosviner et al., "Heroin Use in a Provincial Town" (chap. 1, n. 16 above); J. Zacune, M. Mitcheson, and S. Malone, "Heroin Use in a Provincial Town: One Year Later," *International Journal of the Addictions* 4 (1969): 537-70.

12 De Alarcon, "The Spread of Heroin Abuse in Community" (chap. 1, n. 16 above).

13 R. de Alarcon and N. H. Rathod, "Prevalence and Early Detection of Heroin Abuse" (chap. 6, n. 5 above).

14 R. de Alarcon, "Epidemiological Evaluation of a Public Health Measure Aimed at Reducing the Avail-

ability of Methylamphetamine," *Psychological Medicine* 2 (1972): 293–300.

15   M. Kato, "An Epidemiological Analysis of the Fluctuation of Drug Dependence in Japan," *International Journal of the Addictions* 4 (1969): 591–621; M. Kato, "Epidemiology of Drug Dependence in Japan," in *Drug Abuse Proceedings of the International Conference,* ed. C. J. D. Zarafonetis (Philadelphia: Lea & Febiger, 1972), pp. 67–70.

16   Brill and Hirose report the epidemic involved a total of two million, but the half-million estimate is more consistently used in the literature (see H. Brill and T. Hirose, "The Rise and Fall of a Methamphetamine Epidemic: Japan, 1945–55," *Seminars in Psychiatry,* vol. 1, no. 2 [1969]).

17   Japan Ministry of Health and Welfare, Task Force on Corrections, *A Brief Account of Drug Abuse and Counter Measures in Japan* (1972).

18   N. Motohashi, Head Narcotics Division, Ministry of Health and Welfare, Japan (personal communication, February 1975).

19   One of the reasons suggested for effective case finding in Japan is the national police agency regulation requiring each officer to live in the immediate area of his duty station and to know his community (see New York State 1973 Legislative Document no. 11, *How People Overseas Deal with Drugs* [Albany, 1973]).

20   Japan Ministry of Health and Welfare, *A Brief Account of Drug Abuse.*

Chapter 9

1   C. Hite, "States Fear Data System May Violate Addict Rights," *Psychiatric News* 7, no. 24 (1973): 1, 16; *Client Oriented Data Acquisition Process: National Management Handbook* (Rockville, Md.: National Institute on Drug Abuse, November 1974).

2   L. G. Hunt, *Heroin Epidemics: A Quantitative Study of Current Empirical Data* (Washington, D.C., Drug Abuse Council, May 1973); and Hunt, *Recent Spread*

of Heroin Use in the United States (chap. 7, n. 7
above).

3   In his analysis of heroin spread diagrams from de
Alarcon in England, from Levengood in Detroit, and
from our Chicago studies (see fig. 4 of chap. 6), Hunt
claims that the three epidemics peaked and declined
too rapidly to permit an intervention effort to be
launched. O'Donnell reanalyzed the same data and
feels this pessimistic conclusion is unwarranted because all three sets of data were collected and
reported while the epidemics were presumably still
active. Without additional monitoring it cannot be
assumed that the epidemics had run their course or
even that they had peaked. Hunt's argument is also
based upon his finding that heroin spreaders are
contagious primarily during the first year they use the
drug. This would again make effective intervention
unlikely because a program would have to be extremely sensitive to identify and treat heroin users at
such an early stage of the disorder. But O'Donnell
claims these same data do not show the majority of
heroin introductions as occurring during the first year
of the spreaders' heroin habits. He concludes that
"for more than half of the cases where a longer
interval is conceivable, the data say it may well have
been the case" (see J. O'Donnell, "Onset of Narcotics
Use" [working paper presented to the Second Issues
Conference, sponsored by the U.S. Special Action
Office for Drug Abuse Control and the Drug Abuse
Council, Reston, Va., November 1973]). If the heroin
user is contagious for a longer period than Hunt
suggests, even a not-so-rapid treatment response is
likely to at least partially neutralize the tendency of
some to spread the habit. We should also note that
the three epidemics that were used in Hunt's study,
were exposed to treatment intervention either in
conjunction with or following the data collections
(e.g., our Altgeld intervention), so that they do not
serve as examples of epidemics that have been permitted to run their natural course.

4   See also N. T. J. Bailey, *The Mathematical Theory of
Epidemics* (London: Charles Griffin, 1957).

5   Hughes et al., "Addicts, Police and the Neighborhood Social System" (chap. 2, n. 4 above).

6   Strategy Council on Drug Abuse, *Federal Strategy for Drug Abuse and Drug Traffic Prevention* (Washington, D. C.: Government Printing Office, 1974).

7   On the national level the first effort was the NIMH Conference on the Epidemiology of Drug Abuse, held in February 1973. The National Institute of Drug Abuse sponsored another epidemiological conference in November 1974. In addition, the President's Special Action Office for Drug Abuse Prevention established in 1973 a committee to review epidemiological research issues (see *Operational Definitions in Socio-Behavioral Drug Use Research* [Rockville, Md.: National Institute of Drug Abuse, 1975]). On the international level the World Health Organization's Expert Committee on Drug Dependence met in November 1972 to review the epidemiology of drug dependence (see chap. 2, n. 9 above). The WHO has since initiated an international epidemiological research and reporting program. The WHO Regional Office for Europe also sponsored a conference in September 1972 (see *The Epidemiology of Drug Dependence* [Copenhagen: W.H.O Regional Office for Europe, 1973]).

8   See n. 6 above.

9   Ward, *Employment and Addiction* (chap. 7, n. 13 above).

Index

Abrams, A., 141 n8

Addiction: chronic, 118, 120, 123; and crime, 66–67, 68, 72, 88, 111; in Japan, 114; physician-induced, 113; and race, 59–60, 74, 75. *See also* Dependence, physical; Incidence; Urine test

Addiction control, 118–19, 120, 124; in Japan, 115, 117; neighborhood level, 4, 91–108, 124, 126. *See also* Drug abuse programs; Intervention, treatment; Treatment programs

Addict-prone personality, 57–58

Addicts, xvi, 15, 16–17, 92, 100; interest in treatment, 19–20, 116; number of, 4, 42, 43, 73, 92, 113. *See also* Ex-addicts

Agar, Michael, 27, 137 n8

Alarcon, Richard De, 75, 77, 87, 113, 123, 134 n16, 114 n3, 146 n8, 148 n12, 148 n14, 150 n3; and N. H. Rathod, 113, 144 n5, 148 n13

Alcohol, use of, 81, 85

Alcoholic treatment programs, 126

Aliases, among addicts, 33

Allen, Eugene, 15, 17

Altgeld Gardens, 5, 55–56, 81, 90, 91–108, 127, 145 n4

Altgeld-Murray Community Council, 93, 95, 106, 145 n3; Health Committee of, 94, 106

Altgeld Urban Progress Center, 96

Amphetamine epidemic. *See* Epidemic, amphetamine

Amphetamines, 78, 81, 112, 114

Anderson, G. W., 135 n5

Army, U.S. *See* Drug abuse programs, U.S. Army

Arrests, drug, 61–63, 88, 115–116; records of, 108, 115, 117, 141 n10

"Incubation period," of heroin epidemics, 71–72, 97, 102, 141–42 n11
Informers, 13, 14, 29–30, 33, 39, 63, 138 n12
Initial heroin use. *See* Heroin use, first
Intervention, treatment, 4, 12, 22, 28, 50, 89–90, 104, 123, 124, 128; model for, 73–90, 91; and prevalence, 44, 98–100, 102, 103, 107; projects, 42–46, 48–56, 61, 91–108. *See also* Outreach; Treatment programs
Isolated-case addiction, 75–76, 77, 78

Jaffe, Jerome, xvii, 9, 133–34 n10
Japan, drug abuse programs in, 109–10, 114–16, 117
Japan Ministry of Health and Welfare, 149 n17, 149 n20
Job opportunities, for ex-addicts, 95, 127–28
Johnson, Clyde, 14–15, 17–18
Josephson, E., 148 n6
Judd, L., 146–47 n10
Judicial discretion, 64

Kato, M., 149 n15
Kobrin, Solomon, 59, 140 n4, 141 n9
Koretsky, Sonny, 18
Kosviner, 148 n11

L-alpha-acetylmethadol (LAAM), 8
Larner, J., 26, 137 n2
Law enforcement: and drug use, 12–13, 44, 61–63, 66, 90, 103; and treatment programs, 125–26
Lawson, Clarence. *See* "Sup"
Lexington Federal Narcotics Hospital, 27
Life style, of addicts. *See* Subculture, heroin addict
"Loitering addict" law, 64
Lopez, Rio, 49, 51
LSD, 85

McFarland, R. L., 142 n13
McKay, Henry, 59, 60, 140 n4
Macroepidemic, 75–77, 81–83, 88, 90, 91–108; neighborhoods, 89, 90, 118
Man, the, 17, 135 n8
Marijuana, 60, 61, 63–64, 66, 67, 78, 85
Mass media, response to drug abuse, 66–67, 112, 143 n15
Methadone: diversion to streets, 7; maintenance, 7–8, 99, 100, 112, 116; outpatient clinics, 10, 43, 49;